THE WESTERN FRONTIER LIBRARY

Arctic Schoolteacher

Ed and I in 1930, shortly before going to Alaska

Arctic Schoolteacher

Kulukak, Alaska, 1931–1933

Abbie Morgan Madenwald

University of Oklahoma Press : Norman and London

This book is published with the generous assistance of the Wallace C. Thompson Endowment Fund, University of Oklahoma Foundation.

Library of Congress Cataloging-in-Publication Data

Madenwald, Abbie Morgan, 1908–
   Arctic schoolteacher : Kulukak, Alaska, 1931–1933 / Abbie Morgan Madenwald.
     p. cm.—(The Western frontier library ; 59)
   1. Madenwald, Abbie Morgan, 1908– —Diaries. 2. Teachers—Alaska—Kulukak—Diaries. I. Title. II. Series
LA2317.M24A3 1992
371.1'0092—dc20   92-54129
ISBN: 0–8061–2469–5 (cloth)   CIP
ISBN: 0–8061–2611–6 (paper)

Arctic Schoolteacher: Kulukak,Alaska, 1931–1933 is Volume 59 in The Western Frontier Library.

The paper in this book meets the guidelines for permanence and durability of the Committee on Production Guidelines for book Longevity of the Council on Library Resources, Inc. ∞

3 4 5 6 7 8 9 10 11 12 13 14 15 16 17 18 19 20

This book is dedicated first to Orville, whose interest and encouragement inspired its creation, and to our children, Mary and Malcolm, who grew up with the manuscript. My gratitude to Mary and Dick, whose determination helped to make it all come together.

Contents

Illustrations

Maps

All photographs, unless otherwise credited, were taken by Abbie and Ed Morgan. The film was developed by Ed in the kitchen at Kulukak.

Foreword

This personal account of life in a remote rural Alaskan village is one of several written by teachers who have wished to share their experiences. Until now, however, none has represented the early 1930s in this Bristol Bay area. For those interested in the region, especially Kulukak Bay, this book provides new information not only on school history, but on the area's reindeer herd as well. For Abbie Morgan, the assignment at the U.S. government's territorial station at Kulukak included teaching, while her husband, Ed (who hoped to be a doctor someday), was to provide health care for the village population and monitor the area's reindeer herd. We see how the author and her husband adapted to the physical and social environment, and to a people and language initially strange to them. We also see how Abbie gradually came to appreciate the beauty of the land and its people. The book will be of interest to anyone curious about working or living in communities where English is a foreign or second language, and where an understanding of the local culture is necessary for a successful relationship with the community.

Government records of the U.S. Bureau of Education, under which the Kulukak school and reindeer station were opened, and subsequent bureaus (the Office of Indian Affairs and the Bureau of Indian Affairs) show that 1911–1936 mark the years of the school's existence at Kulukak.[1] Bristol Bay oral history accounts from the ANCSA (Alaska Native Claims Settlement Act) 14 (h) (1) historical and cemetery sites project of the Bureau of Indian Affairs, ANCSA Office in Anchorage, Alaska, show school construction beginning during the summer of 1911, and students attending that fall.[2]

Robert Kallenberg was the teacher at Kulukak during the 1926–1927 school year and is now eighty-seven years old and residing near Anchorage. He accepted the assignment to teach there because of his interest in the reindeer service, and first arrived in Dillingham during the summer of 1926. He worked at the orphanage in Kanakanak until he could get a boat to take him around Cape Constantine, and finally reached the Kulukak station in September. There he discovered that the school had not been able to retain a teacher since 1919, largely because of the nomadic lifestyle of the people. Children simply did not stay in school. Patusia Alakayak of Manokotak said in an interview for the BIA-ANCSA 14(h) (1) project that "the [Kulukak] school was built in 1911 and we stayed for five years until the teachers stopped coming" (BIA-ANCSA-84TOG01).[3] In the spring of 1927, when Kallenberg found that his students all had gone with their families to Jack Cove for herring fishing, he moved to the Dillingham area, where he stayed for years.

Once schools had begun to be established in the region, people were eager for the new opportunity to have their children educated. Some families would send their children to stay with relatives in places where schools were established, but many preferred to keep their families intact. At the time the Morgans arrived at their assigned station, the owner of the reindeer herd was

Peter Krause, who had originally settled with his family in Kulukak because of the school. He continued to manage the Kulukak herd until packs of wolves chased the deer, killing some, which made control of the remaining animals impossible. These events are reported in unpublished texts of interviews in 1979 and with one of Krause's herders, John Gumlickpuk of New Stuyahok and in the 1984 BIA-ANCSA interviews. Nellie Ilutsik Coolidge confirmed the reports in recent interviews with elders in Dillingham. The summer after Ed Morgan's death, Krause moved with his family to Lake Aleknagik, where a school was opening. Others from Kulukak, including George Ilutsik, one of Abbie Morgan's students, also moved there. Ilutsik, who had been raised by Krause's mother, eventually brought up his own family in Aleknagik.

The ANCSA 14(h) (1) interviews confirm that school closure occurred around the time the reindeer herds were wiped out, 1935–1936.[4] Kulukak Village no longer exists, and people going to the bay usually camp away from the abandoned site.

In preparing Abbie Morgan Madenwald's manuscript for publication, the editors tried to remain true to her text, and we believe the work reflects her personal character throughout. Other than the usual editorial procedures, we made few changes. What emerges as important in the book is the human drama, and the extent to which Abbie managed to overcome the prejudices of her time.

We have substituted modern Yup'ik orthography for Eskimo words that were spelled by Abbie as she originally had recorded them. (Yup'ik is the language of the Central Yup'ik Eskimos spoken in southwestern Alaska in the Yukon-Kuskokwim Delta and Bristol Bay areas (see map on p. xvi). Translations are given upon the first occurrence of a Yup'ik term. Out of respect for Abbie's efforts to work with the language, however,

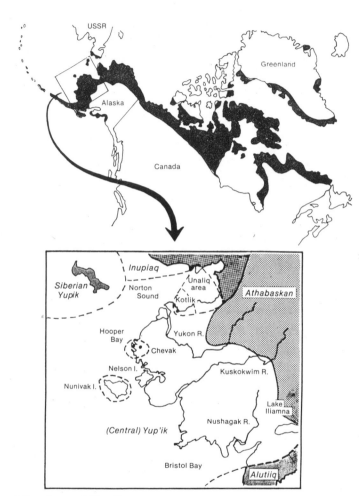

The Central Yup'ik region of western Alaska, showing the dialect areas. From *Yup'ik Eskimo Dictionary*, by Steven A. Jacobson. Courtesy of Alaska Native Language Center, University of Alaska Fairbanks.

we also present below the transcriptions as they appeared in her original manuscript; a simple pronunciation guide is included.

Although a detailed description of the modern Yup'ik orthography is not necessary here, it is useful to comment on those consonants that have no equivalent sound in English. The stop consonants, *p, t,* and *k* are much as in English. The *c,* which is never pronounced like the English *k,* is similar to the English *ch.* The *q* is pronounced farther back in the mouth than is the *k,* with the back of the tongue against the soft palate rather than the hard palate. In the English approximations below, an italicized *k* or *ck* represents the *q* sound. The consonant *g* is like the Greek γ, and the *r* is somewhat like the German uvular *r.* Next to stop consonants, the *g* and *r* are voiceless, and are capitalized in the pronunciation guide below.

Modern Yup'ik orthography	Abbie Morgan Madenwald's original form	Pronunciation guide
aang	ong	ahng
akutaq	a-goo-tuk	ah-**koo**-tu*ck*
assiituq	i-see-tuk	ahs-**see**-to*ke*
assirtuq	asuktuk	ah-**siR**-to*ke*
cama-i	chemi, chimi, chi-mi	chum-**eye**
carayak	shagiak	cha-**rah**-yuck
cukamek	cha-gum-uk	chew-**kah**-mek
kelipaq	kli-puk	**klee**-pu*ck*
naamikika	now-ma-keek	**nah**-me-**kee**-kah
piivaq	bee-wak	**bee**-wu*ck*
qalirtaq	kaliktuk	*k*ah-*liR*-tu*ck*
qang'a	konga	**kahng**-ngah
qasgiq	kazkik	*k*uz-gi*ck*
qemitaanritek	kamitartook	*k*e-**mee-taan**-ri-tek
Qimugteq	Camooktuk	*k*e-**mooG**-te*ck*
quyana	kuyana, ku-yana	*k*o-**yah**-nah
suungcautet	soon-chow-dit	**soong-chow**-tet
taitai	ti ti	**tie**-tie
tepet	titmuk, titnek	t-pet
uluaq	ulu	**ool**-loo-u*ck*

When loan words are used in Yup'ik speech, an -*aq* or -*ar* frequently is added to the borrowed word, as in *skuulaq* (school) or *skuularista* (teacher). (Note that we have retained Abbie's spelling *schoolarista* for the latter.)

When a Yup'ik word such as *carayak* (spirit) is used in English speech, and a plural form is desired, it is common to add a simple English plural marking, thus *carayaks* instead of *carayiit* and *schoolaristas* instead of *skuularistet*.

Some italicized words in the text, such as *tyone* (chief) and *barabara* (sod dwelling), are not Yup'ik in origin, having come to Alaska from the opposite side of the Bering Sea. Words that were borrowed from Eskimo languages and have become standard English are not italicized. Examples of these are "kayak" (from *qayaq*) and "mukluk" (borrowed into English for "Eskimo skin boots" from the word for bearded seal, *maklak,* the skin of which was used for the soles of such boots).

Place names and personal names are presented in Anglicized form—for example, Kulukak for the Yup'ik Quluqaq and Togiak for Tuyuryaraq—so as to maintain consistency with maps, personal records, and documents from schools, government agencies, and churches. The author provided a roster, which she called "Children in the Classroom," with names written as they would probably be in school records. In the list below, Yup'ik orthography for family names is given in brackets. This is for purposes of identification only; the individuals did not spell their names this way. Perhaps ten of these people are living today, several having remained all their lives in the Bristol Bay region.

Children in the Classroom

Seven little girls:	Matrona Aigogiyuwak [Akagyuguaq]
	Mollia Kasuchta [Quserta]
	Sassa Polleskuyea [Pilayuilnguq]
	Grace Krause
	Olia Krause
	Elsie Inglosok [Inglussuk]
	Mary Inglosok [Inglussuk]
Five little boys:	Christian Yukeyak [Yugiiyaq]
	Michael Kasuchta [Quserta]
	Step-han Aigogiyuwak [Akagyuguaq]
	Gus Polleskuyea [Pilayuilnguq]
	George Krause
Eight older girls:	Anecia Aigogiyuwak [Akagyuguaq]
	Sophia Aigogiyuwak [Akagyuguaq]
	Ocalena Chakookwylnok [Cakulluilnquq]
	Sophia Chakookwylnok [Cakulluilnquq]
	Annie Gusuklaulra [Qasiaqalria]
	Lucy Gusuklaulra [Qasiaqalria]
	Annie Krause
	Nattia Polleskuyea [Pilayuilnguq]
Reindeer herders (often absent because of time spent with the reindeer):	
	George Ilutsik [Lerelcuk]
	Charlie Chickonook [Cukanaq]
	Jimmie Aigogiyuwak [Akagyuguaq]
	Andrewski

Special thanks are due Tom Alton, editor at the Alaska Native Language Center at the University of Alaska Fairbanks, for his generous editorial assistance.

I am very grateful to two of George and Lena Ilutsik's daughters, Nellie Ilutsik Coolidge and Esther Abbie Ilutsik, for their assistance in reviewing the manuscript. Nellie has frequently been associated with my Yup'ik language research over the years, and Esther's

comments on the manuscript were very helpful. Esther's middle name was chosen by her father in memory
of his teacher Abbie Morgan, with hopes that his daughter would also choose education as a profession. She did.

IRENE REED

Fairbanks, Alaska
February 1991

Notes

1. *Historical Status of Elementary Schools in Rural Alaskan Communities, 1867–1860,* by Carol Barnhardt, Center
for Cross-Cultural Studies, University of Alaska Fairbanks,
1985. (Shows Kulukak as "Kularak.")

2. From tapes and transcripts of ANCSA 14(h) (1) interviews conducted in August 1984 by BIA-ANCSA Offices, Anchorage, Alaska; Tom Brosig and Fred Harden, interviewers;
Martha Lockuk, Peter Lockuk, and Anecia Lomack, interpret-
ers; BIA-ANCSA-84TOG01, with Patusia Alakayak of Manokotak and BIA-ANCSA-84TOG04-06, with Andrew and Tom
Bavilla and Tom Chythlook of Aleknagik, ANLC transcriptions and translations from Yup'ik by Marie Meade, Alaska
Native Language Center.

3. Ibid.

4. Ibid.

Books of Interest

Fienup-Riordan, Ann. *The Nelson Island Eskimo: Social Structure
    and Ritual Distribution.* Anchorage: Alaska Pacific University
    Press, 1983. Includes descriptions of traditional customs in modern
    Yup'ik culture.
Jacobson, Steven A. *Central Yup'ik and the Schools.* Juneau: Alaska
    Department of Education, Bilingual/Bicultural Program, 1984. A
    handbook for teachers.
———. *Yup'ik Eskimo Dictionary.* Fairbanks: Alaska Native Lan-
    guage Center, University of Alaska, 1984. Covers the entire Cen-
    tral Yup'ik language with all its dialects; a full introduction in-
    cludes a description of the sound and writing systems.
Nelson, Edward W. *The Eskimos About Bering Strait.* Bureau of

American Ethnology Annual Report. Vol. 1, pp. 1–518. 1899. Reprint. Washington, D.C.: Smithsonian Institution, 1983. Provides extensive nineteenth century documentation of Yup'ik culture and technology.

Oswalt, Wendell H. *Alaskan Eskimos*. San Francisco: Chandler Publishing Co., 1967. A general anthropological survey concentrating on pre-European-contact culture and technology.

Reed, E. Irene, Osahito Miyaoka, Steven Jacobson, Paschal Afcan, and Michael Krauss. *Yup'ik Eskimo Grammar*. Fairbanks: Alaska Native Language Center and Yup'ik Language Workshop, 1977. The present standard grammar of the language, arranged as a two-and-a-half year college-level course in Yup'ik, with exercises and extensive bibliography of work in the language published before 1977.

VanStone, James W. *Eskimos of the Nushagak River*. Seattle and London, University of Washington Press, 1967. An excellent ethnographic history of the Nushagak River region on Bristol Bay, with an emphasis on culture change among the Eskimos under impact of growing contact with the outside world.

Vick, Ann, ed. *The Cama-i Book*. Garden City, N.Y.: Anchor Books, 1983. Personal histories and ways of life, collected by high school students for a Foxfire project.

Preface

In 1931 my mother and her first husband were living in eastern Washington, near Palouse, where Mom taught in the one-room school and Ed worked in the wheat fields earning money to save for medical school. They lived in a cottage on the school grounds. The economy was in depression and the couple's financial future looked bleak. When offered contracts as part of the U.S. government's program to send teachers to remote areas to educate, train, and offer medical aid to the Native population in Alaska Territory, they debated briefly, then eagerly signed.

Mom's responsibility was to be the *schoolarista,* teaching the children of the village as well as the adults. Ed was to provide basic medical care, help the people any way he could, and monitor the reindeer herd that ranged nearby.

From the adventure's first mention in Palouse, Mom kept an extensive diary and later wrote a book-length manuscript of her experiences in a Yup'ik Eskimo society that in 1931 was still relatively unchanged by Western ways.

It is rare and unique material from which to draw. A number of the villagers had never seen a white woman.

The children were eager and receptive to the couple who came to the station with humor, a new language, candy, and a dog that was allowed in the house and who wore denim boots on the ice.

With respectful understanding, Mom tells of the innate ability of the Eskimos to survive the harsh environment. She admired their resourcefulness and determination, and the happiness of the children and their families is a quality that shines through. This dramatic tale of adventure is told with admiration, love, and respect, and provides priceless insight into a society that few of us will ever experience.

Mom and Ed were the Peace Corps of their time, dedicating themselves to participating in a culture in transition. This dedication was given at considerable personal sacrifice.

MARY MADENWALD McKEOWN

Moraga, California
February 1992

Author's Note

This manuscript was written over a span of years. My children grew up with the stories of Kulukak, the continuing friendship of Ocalena, and the deadlines my writing classes demanded.

Mary would sit by my desk, reading and rereading the pages as they came from my typewriter, and after twenty years of seeing the manuscript on my closet shelf, said it was what she wanted most for Christmas. I sent it to her immediately, delighted she still cared for it, and I am pleased beyond measure at this end result.

ABBIE MORGAN MADENWALD

1908–1991

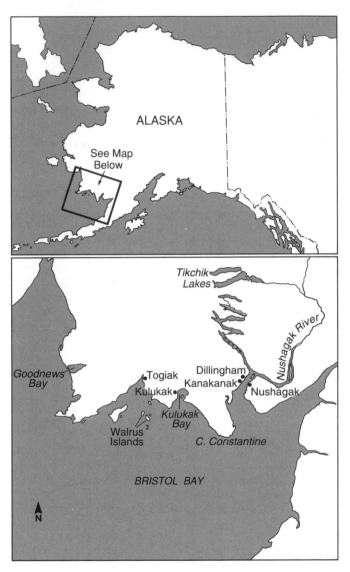

Southwestern Alaska (bottom). Top map shows position of
southwestern Alaska within the state.

Arctic Schoolteacher

1. Tundra Bound

As the SS *Aleutian,* Alaska bound, pulled away from the Seattle pier that August day in 1931, I glanced at my husband and his happiness melted my misgivings. It mattered little that Ed and I were leaving family and friends behind and that his college course was incomplete. We and Spike, our German shepherd, were heading for the remote, isolated Eskimo village of Kulukak on Bristol Bay, an arm of the Bering Sea. We had jobs as U.S. government teachers, and would be the only white people within a radius of sixty miles.

The ten days since the telegram had arrived at our cottage by the school in Washington State's Palouse country had been tense and confused. I had planned to teach another year while Ed finished work toward his degree at Washington State University.

That telegram had upset it all.

Before Ed had raised his serious gray eyes from the message, I knew we were going to Alaska. Anticipation and determination showed through the lines of weariness that summer days spent in the heat of the wheat fields had worn on his face.

That evening we sat at the kitchen table with a sheet of paper before us and Spike asleep at our feet. Ed drew

3

a line down the center and labeled one side "For" and the other "Against." The first item on the "For" side was "Hopelessness of finding work in the States during the Depression years." Ed's goal was the study of medicine, and he hoped that if we spent two or three years in Alaska, we would save enough money to carry him through medical school. Also in the "For" column he wrote in big letters, "ADVENTURE—frontier country."

On the "Against" side he wrote "No. 1" and looked questioningly at me. Suddenly the cautious side was all mine. Resting my elbows on the table, I counted with my fingers. "Number one, distance from our families. Number two, the three credits you lack for your degree. Number three, the contract I signed to teach here next year."

We need not have listed those items. We knew we were on our way.

After several exchanges of telegrams, Ed arranged to complete his college work by correspondence. I made a hesitant trip to see the members of the school board and requested a release from my contract. We packed hurriedly and journeyed across the state to our families at Grays Harbor. A crazy week of confusion followed, in which we bought wool underclothing in the heat of the summer and dashed to Seattle to buy a year's supply of food—canned chickens and hams, powdered milk, butter in kegs, bacon in tins, dried eggs and eggs sealed in wax, popcorn, and Christmas candy. How much flour do you buy for a year? How much did it take for one baking of bread? And how much coffee at a pound a week? I staggered under the total. We'd have to remain in Alaska for the rest of our days to pay the grocery bill.

Food was my department, and Ed waited patiently as I worried about flour, shortening, and sugar. As we left the wholesale grocer's, he looked at the street signs. "Now for film developing equipment, a gun, and ammunition." We combined forces in the choice of books and a radio.

Ed reminded me that we would be the only non-Eskimos in an area larger than Rhode Island.

Our families waved a last good-bye. Ed's consisted of his father, while mine included parents, a sister, and a grandmother to whom I was especially devoted. The family was impatient with such rashness as this Alaska idea, having already suffered enough anxiety over my cousin Edgar, who had gone to Alaska to fish for a summer, but had remained to trap that winter and to fish for another summer. At Grandmother's insistence that he return immediately to complete his education, Edgar, with apologies to poet Robert Service, airmailed the following lines:

> The strong life that never knows harness,
>   The wilds where the caribou call,
> The freshness, the freedom, the farness,
>   Oh God how I'm stuck on it all.
> (Robert W. Service, "The Spell of the Yukon")

Edgar's letter was postmarked Dillingham. The last telegram his mother received had been sent from the radio station at Kanakanak, the government industrial school and orphanage on the Nushagak River near Dillingham and the last stop on our journey to Kulukuk. Grandmother, picturing us in the bleak, barren wasteland, found comfort in the thought of the three of us together.

The days on board ship were timeless and tranquil. We danced by moonlight, relaxed in deck chairs as the ship glided through the Inside Passage, and watched the wooded mountains reach from the water's edge. Lonely totem poles stood vigil among the trees. We enjoyed the motion of the ship as it plowed through the blue waters.

In Juneau an official of the Bureau of Indian Affairs, U.S. Department of the Interior, met us.

"School will be in session seven months a year," he said. "You're to render what medical aid you can to the villagers. Medicines were delivered to Kulukak in the spring by the government supply ship."

And to Ed's chagrin, he added, "There's a reindeer herd at Kulukak, which will be under your supervision." All Ed knew about reindeer was what he'd seen on Christmas cards.

Seward marked the end of the run for the SS *Aleutian,* and a stopover of several days. At the hotel we met Ted, short for Theodosia McConnell, whose destination was Kanakanak, where she would assume duties as matron for the boys' dormitory. We spent many happy and profitable hours with her, gleaning valuable information from her store of experience in Alaska.

I looked up to meet Ed's discerning eyes as our watches were set back two hours, and I put into words what he knew was in my thoughts. "We're a long, long way from home."

At dusk one evening we left by mailboat to sail southwest down the Alaska Peninsula to Dutch Harbor, then northeast into the Bering Sea, on to Bristol Bay, and up the Nushagak River to Dillingham and Kanakanak.

As we boarded the SS *Starr,* the purser inquired about our dog.

"The fare for a dog is twenty-one dollars," he said.

I protested, "We paid eleven dollars on the SS *Aleutian,* and at the time were told we'd have to pay an additional ten dollars when we boarded this boat."

"The fare is twenty-one dollars."

Hotel and meals in Seward and the few souvenirs sent to the family had left us without twenty-one dollars between us. Spike stood on deck, wagging his tail trustingly.

The SS *Starr*. Ed and I huddled by the smokestack.

Ted opened her bag and counted her money, but even with her help we couldn't come up with twenty-one dollars. Ted was a practical person, and to her, a dog was a dog. I was startled to hear her suggest, "Why don't you just dispose of the dog? You can always get another."

I battled tears. Just then the captain appeared and took in the situation.

"All right, all right," he said. "We make it ten dollars den."

That night the little boat rolled and tossed and pitched, and it was cold. I lay in my shelf-bunk below

Ed's, closed my eyes and shuddered as clothes swung back and forth from their hooks and furniture slid and banged.

A day finally came when the seas quieted. Ted, Ed, and I sat huddled by the smokestack with Vi Frenz, a nurse for the Kanakanak hospital. Decks were piled high with boxes, barrels, lumber, and sacks of coal. Snow-capped mountains loomed along the peninsula, and there was a fresh, invigorating quality to the air. Whales and porpoises frolicked about us. The weather grew colder, and strong winds whipped our scarves, forcing us to button our coats and tuck our hands in our pockets. The shoreline was gray and indistinct in either evening haze or morning fog.

The captain told Ed at lunch one day that "city dogs" have much to learn in Alaska. "To your dog, when he got in my way, I said, 'Mush!' He yoost sit and lick his chops." With the thoughts of the Kulukak reindeer herd weighing heavily on his mind, Ed told the captain, "City dogs and city dudes have a hell of a lot to learn in this country."

A tall, swarthy, Italian aviator, who wore a beret and a long coat of foreign cut, was making a boat trip preliminary to a flight. He spoke little English and eagerly tried to learn, pointing at objects and then staring inquiringly at anyone nearby. At mealtimes he wanted to be told the names of various foods. Once, while he held up the jam dish, the ship was rolling in heavy seas and no one felt sociable. In exasperation, the captain barked out, "Yam, man, yam!" Before we reached False Pass, we knew just what the Italian wanted when we heard "yelly," "yuice," or "yohhnny cake."

A precocious, pigtailed Eskimo girl of eight or nine traveled alone to the orphanage at Kanakanak. She drifted in and out of steerage, above and below decks, and in and out of the galley. One evening as we seated ourselves at dinner, she announced, "There's cock-roaches in the galley."

I wouldn't have known a cockroach from a bumble bee, and with no choice of restaurants, I dismissed it from my thoughts. Later, across the table, Ted stared with abhorrence at her plate. She put down her fork, our eyes met, and she answered my unspoken question with a nod. Quickly, I swallowed the potatoes in my mouth, lumps and all. I looked at Ed, who was talking with the captain. I glanced at his plate and saw that the potatoes were gone. Ted's eyes met mine again, and we kept our secret to ourselves.

At Dutch Harbor a letter from our district superintendent was delivered to Ed. A launch was to take us and our supplies from Kanakanak to Kulukak, a distance of one hundred miles by boat, with a stopover of several days at the industrial school.

Oh, I hope there's time to get word to and from our families and to locate Cousin Edgar, I thought.

With apprehension, we learned that the last lap of our journey was an extremely hazardous passage through the waters off Cape Constantine.

2. Kanakanak

Anchoring in the heavy swell, the mailboat blew her throaty blast in the dismal dawn. Ted, Vi, Ed, and I were the last of the passengers. We stood with Spike in the wind and rain and peered across the gray waters of the Nushagak. Somewhere on that distant shore was Kanakanak, and Vi eagerly hoped for a glimpse of the settlement where she was to live and work. She pointed toward the shore, and we watched a launch making its way toward us, battling the wind and waves.

Noisily, the crew piled boxes and crates on board, rolled barrels, carried sacks, and stowed them near the rails. For the little steamer, this was the end of the line, her last call before the river became icebound. Tonight's ebbing tide would find her plowing back to the waters of Bristol Bay, heading west to south and slipping from the near-Arctic.

The launch drew alongside, and a man in a rain parka waved and shouted as the boat rode the swells. "We'll take the passengers in, then bring out the lighter and start unloading," he said.

One at a time, we climbed cautiously down the Jacob's ladder, dropping into the launch. A member of the crew gave Ed a helping hand with Spike, who vociferously suffered the indignity of being carried. Now that we were leaving her, and rolling and pitching in a smaller boat, the steamer didn't seem so little after all. Above the gray walls of her sides, we had known a security I no longer felt. From where we looked, she was stately and grand, easily and confidently riding at anchor.

Rain and spray soaked us, and Spike whined uneasily. Vi shook her head, fighting down the nausea that had plagued her the entire trip. Ted's confident smile was reassuring to us as we headed from crest into trough and back up to crest. Her expression implied that this experience was trivial in a frontier country.

Ed wore a broad smile as he held Spike's collar. He winked at me, saying without words, "This is the life."

Gradually we drew closer to the shore, and the grayness of the land became green. Buildings were scattered on the distant hill. A group of people stood on the ridge as the launch slowed, turned, and pulled up before the mud bank. The arrival of the mailboat with new faces from the Outside was evidently occasion enough to rise early, tramp down to the beach, and wait in the wet cold.

Vi, Ted, and I were aware of our audience as we, in turn, jumped from the gunwale of the launch to a toehold on the mud bank and were pulled by helping hands from above and pushed by Ed from below onto the trail that marked the end of the journey for Vi and Ted.

"Welcome to Kanakanak," shouted a handsome man dressed in a long coat reminiscent of the type worn by Russian Cossacks. Who was the nurse? Who was the matron for the boys' dormitory? Who were the Kulukak teachers? All the members of the little group were connected to the industrial school. They were teachers, nurses, cooks, engineers, maintenance workers, and radio operators. The Cossack, we learned, was the school's superintendent.

He nodded toward a smiling man of perhaps twenty-

eight and said, "Mr. Mason here spent last year at
Kulukak. He wants to sell you his supply of groceries.
You'll have a lot to talk about." The man spoke so
rapidly and with such a peculiar accent that I found it
difficult to follow him. Mr. Mason shook hands heartily,
removing his cap and exposing a prematurely bald head
above a smiling face. To look at him was to like him.

We made our way single file up a two-plank walk
bordered by dripping shrubs. Ed forthrightly asked the
question uppermost in our minds. "Do you know when
we leave for Kulukak?" I was anxiously hoping, in bliss-
ful ignorance, that we'd be in Kanakanak at least long
enough to send a wire to Grandmother and to receive a
reply.

"A man by the name of Penny was engaged to take
you," the Cossack said, "but yesterday he backed out.
There's a bad stretch of water between here and Kulukak. Everyone's afraid of it because of the tide rips and
treacherous reefs off the cape."

How else can we get there?" Ed asked.

"I suggest you wire your district superintendent at
Dutch Harbor. There have been transportation diffi-
culties in former years. He'll advise you."

Mr. Mason spoke up. "Chris, an Eskimo trader from
Togiak, the village beyond Kulukak, brought me over
this spring. He said he'd take me back this fall when
he came over for his supplies."

He explained that he had come to Kanakanak for the
summer but had been transferred permanently to the
industrial school. "I have to get back to Kulukak for my
clothes and belongings. I know Chris will take all of us
and your provisions, then bring me back and pick up
his supplies."

"When will he be here?" Ed asked.

"No idea. People up here never hurry. But I feel safer
traveling around the cape with him than with any white
man. He makes the trip twice a year and knows those

waters better than anyone. He won't be able to travel much longer by boat this year, so he'll appear any day now."

From farther down the line a man said, "You can't depend on the Eskimos. He might have changed his mind, or maybe he's wrecked his boat. My guess is he won't be here, and if he does come, he'll be stretching his luck trying to make two trips."

The superintendent took Ed and me to a boxlike green building he called the staff house. "We'll put you up in the girls' building, but you'll eat your meals here. It's very nice to have guests with us."

Vi would stay there in the staff house also, and Ted would have an apartment in the boys' dormitory.

The scalding coffee, warm doughnuts, friendly companionship, and steady floor beneath us were wonderful. We were served by shy Eskimo girls in white uniforms and lumpy brown stockings.

A plant in the window was the only color in a room with a plain wooden table and chairs, a brown linoleum floor, and chalk-white walls and curtains. The only luxury was a phonograph in the corner.

Talk around the table was of unloading the mailboat, storing our provisions temporarily, and hauling up the industrial school's supplies by tractor.

Ed turned to the superintendent. "If I can borrow some work clothes, I'd be glad to lend a hand," he said. He and Mr. Mason, or Mace, as he was called, left the room and reappeared with my husband looking like a deckhand. Spike, from beside my chair, eyed him critically.

Mace went with us to the girls' dormitory, where we met the matron, Mrs. Borland. She was a friendly little white-haired woman and the wife of the school's doctor. There was an aroma of freshly baked bread, steamy laundry, and scrubbed wood floors. Mrs. Borland led us up a broad flight of stairs to a plain little room with a dresser, an iron bedstead, and, I was sure, no heat. A naked light bulb dangled from the ceiling. I wondered if there were any color but white in this dismal country.

"The bathroom available to you will be the one in my apartment directly below," the matron told me. "There is a tub, but water must be heated on the range, so you'll have to let me know in advance when you want to take a bath."

Ed and Mace left for the beach while Spike and I went in search of the radio station. A number of green buildings stood at various angles on the grounds. We learned later that a cannery had donated them to the government for use as an orphanage. We learned, too, that they were poorly constructed and that heat poured through the walls as fast as it was created by the heating plant. Two-plank sidewalks connected the buildings—staff house, girls' and boys' dormitories, school, hospital, gymnasium, radio station, and sleeping quarters for some of the employees. Shrubs had been placed as a child drops blocks on a floor. A dismal pall hung over everything. I knew the river was beyond the ridge, but even the mailboat was obscured by fog.

What would we find at Kulukak? Mace had said that he would show us pictures of the village that evening and tell us all he could about it.

I sent a wire to our district superintendent and one to the family, wording it carefully so the homesickness wouldn't show through. That morning we had asked the operator, Mr. Slumberger, if he knew my cousin Edgar Haley.

"Haley, Haley," he said, bouncing his pencil on its eraser. "Yes, he sent some wires here a while back, and returned a few days later for replies. Ask around. He probably isn't far away."

He came to the door with me and pointed me toward the boys' dormitory. Ted greeted me there with a towel pinned around her head, another around her waist, and her sleeves rolled up. As we sat in her living room enjoying cups of coffee, a soft tap sounded on the door and a demure little fellow of perhaps four slipped into the room and stood worshipfully before Ted.

"This is my little friend, my youngest charge," she said.

"Hello," I said. "What is your name?"

"Step-han Jack Mettie Mr. Slumberger Mrs. McConnell," he said. Ted explained that he added the names of people he loved to his own name. Mr. Slumberger often brought him candy, and Ted McConnell was his new mother.

At that moment I felt that I had something in common with little orphan Step-han. I made a mental note to find something for him before I dropped in again. Spike trotted to him and ran a loving, wet tongue up his arm. Step-han Jack Mettie Mr. Slumberger Mrs. McConnell stood hesitantly, wondering about the dog's intentions. Glancing at Ted, he got the reassurance he needed. He reached out and hugged the animal while Spike's tail fanned the air furiously.

That evening in Mace's little upstairs room—also chalk-white and cold—we saw pictures of Kulukak showing the school and living quarters, the *barabaras* (sod dwellings) of the Eskimos, and Peter Krause, a Kulukak villager of mixed ancestry.

"You'll love it," Mace said. "I'd never have left but for the loneliness and the isolation. It isn't good to live alone year after year."

He gave us his grocery list to compare with ours so we could decide if we wanted to buy any of his provisions. He had ordered supplies early in the spring, before he knew he would be transferred to Kanakanak. On the mailboat Ted had expressed misgivings about what she called our "limited supply." We felt we should purchase Mace's groceries, for what we didn't use that year we would use the next or sell to our successor.

We left Mace to return to our room before the electric plant was turned off at ten o'clock, feeling more anxious than ever to get to Kulukak. I fell asleep with Mace's words going through my mind: "Snug, cozy little house on a hill overlooking the harbor. You'll be happy there."

The following day an answer came from our district superintendent, advising the industrial school supervisor to make inquiries about transportation for us. We waited anxiously and impatiently.

On the third day, a reply came from our families. All was well at home. Grandmother was busily knitting wool stockings for us, and everyone sent their best wishes for the remaining part of the journey and safe arrival at Kulukak.

At lunch one day the following week, the superintendent told us that if we couldn't get to Kulukak by boat, in a couple of months we could go by dogsled. Of course, we wouldn't be able to take our provisions or radio, but Mace's supplies would see us through for some time. Kulukak teachers had traveled by dogsled a couple of times in the past. The long idle days were unbearable in the cold little room. For weeks we had been living out of suitcases, and I was most eager to be settled in a place of our own.

That night I told Ed, "God doesn't hear prayers way up here."

At the end of another week, our hopes soared. We found a man who had a boat large enough to carry our provisions, but the motor needed repairs. Another week dragged by, and one morning we were dismayed to find the ground covered with snow.

We waited, hoping each night that the following day would find us on our way to Kulukak. I kept everything ready to go on a moment's notice, but our hopes faded again when the owner of the boat came to the staff house to tell us that he had decided against making the trip. It was too risky traveling so late in the fall, and he might not have been able to make it back into the Nushagak.

Mr. Slumberger—whom we all called Slum—laughed at my impatience. "Alaska is the land of day after tomorrow," he said. "Nobody hurries here. It's a rare treat for us to have guests. Be content to stay as long as you can. You'll have many months of hibernation at Kulukak, and you'll long to see us again."

I spent my days restlessly in the cold, bleak little room and in Ted's apartment. Ed moved our radio there, and a group of us, usually ten or more, gathered evenings to listen to the music and news broadcasts from Outside. We sat in the lamplight into the small hours, lingering over coffee and sandwiches at midnight, sometimes reading mail that had come on a late plane.

Spike slept in our room, stretched out after a full day of playing with youngsters from the orphanage. He was living on dried fish and was as thin as a whippet. I was sure it was his inherent prudence, and not cowardice, that kept him away from the sled dogs. We had been warned that we would lose him if he ever tangled with one of those handsome, vicious creatures. Spike must have overheard. For protection, we got him a wide, heavily studded leather collar.

I asked everyone I met for news of my cousin, but his name was familiar only to Mr. Slumberger at the radio station. It was exasperating to know that Edgar had sent and received messages recently from Kanakanak but had completely disappeared. Slum took delight in teasing me about this.

"There's a new 'squaw man' down the river, and, as I recall, his name is Edgar."

A few days before Slum made this remark, I had been at the hospital with Vi and was introduced to a tall, distinguished man who wore the warm, casual clothes of someone who spends most of his time outdoors. When he left, I asked someone if he worked at the industrial school. For an answer, I was motioned to the window from which I saw him leaving with a little Eskimo woman. She carried a child on her back while two others clung to her skirts.

"Squaw man," it was said of him. "He missed too many boats."

Time dragged, and I tried to reconcile myself to the possibility of remaining in Kanakanak for perhaps a couple more months. We were relieved to learn that Ed's salary had started, for he was on a twelve-month schedule. (My own pay was based on the seven-month school year.) I helped Ted with everything I could. I wrote fat letters to the family. I dawdled over tidying our room, and took Spike for long walks. I read every book I could find. Ed talked of moving our trunks closer to where we would be able to get more clothes. Three times a day we walked single file on the narrow planks to the staff house for meals. At dinner the superintendent's wife kept the phonograph blaring out one scratchy record after another. "Please pass the potatoes," or "May I have the sugar, please?" was said quickly between the "Nutcracker Suite" and the "Volga Boatman."

One evening at dinner, Mace was called to the door. A few moments later, with a triumphant smile on his face, he dashed back in with Chris from Togiak, the tallest Eskimo we had seen. He stood with his feet spread wide and his shoulders slouched forward. Smiling broadly and fingering his fur cap, he called us the new *schoolaristas*. He would take us and our supplies to Kulukak and bring Mace back, he said, but we'd have to "hurry like hell."

"Tomorrow, afternoon tide."

"We'll be ready."

We packed that evening and arranged to take food for several meals. I wrote a last letter to the family, then three to Cousin Edgar. One was to be left with

Slum at the radio station, another at the Dillingham
Post Office, and the third at the general store at Snag
Point, up the Nushagak, telling him we were in
Kulukak and extending a warm and urgent invitation
to visit us.

3. Cape Constantine

Chris's thirty-two foot power boat bobbed on her mooring hawsers while a steady gale swept over the Nushagak. Early fall and late afternoon combined to hold a piercing cold in the air. Mace, Ed, and I hurriedly said good-bye to our friends and boarded the heavily loaded boat. The gunwales were dangerously close to the surface of the water, and I had a sudden, desperate longing to turn back. Even Spike seemed to sense that he was embarking on a trying trip.

Spray was flying over the bow, and Ed, glancing at my wool coat, said, "You'd better climb down inside the cabin. There'll be no way to dry wet clothes."

Envying the men in their slickers, I left the deck with Spike at my heels. The little cabin was dark and stuffy, the ceiling so low I could not stand, the portholes few and tiny, the glass so dirty I could see only dim light through them. The cabin reeked of oil and gasoline from the engine, of stale tobacco smoke from Chris's pipe, of fish, and of the Eskimos' yeasty brew. The room was so crowded that I wondered how four of us would find accommodations of any kind. Our entire year's supply of groceries—cases of canned goods, crates of potatoes, onions, and eggs—along with our trunks and suitcases, filled every available space. But that wasn't all.

"Ivan! Andrewski!" Chris shouted.

I was startled to hear answers from the corner behind the engine, and faintly made out the forms of two Eskimo youths. To my surprise, there would be six of us instead of four. The boys, answering Chris in a language completely unfamiliar to us, scrambled up on deck.

Ed slipped down inside the cabin, his face wet and red from the cold. Spike thumped his tail on the floorboards.

"The wind's changing," he said. "Chris is heading for shelter in a cove called Mud Lagoon. He says we'll stay there tonight, perhaps moving tomorrow, depending on the wind."

Soon the boat jarred as it ran aground and Chris dropped the anchor. Mud Lagoon. How aptly named! For mile upon mile stretched slimy, gray mud, broken only by an occasional clump of swamp grass.

Night came, and with it the problem of where each might make a bed. Ed and Mace slept on the floor in blankets. My bed was Mace's sleeping bag placed on the steamer trunk against the boxes of supplies. Spike, part of the time, served as my pillow, and I, part of the time, served as his. Chris's bed was made up of three gasoline cases placed end to end; his worn squirrelskin parka was his only blanket. The boys were on the floor behind the engine, sandwiched between reindeer skins.

My trunk bed was almost unbearably hard. From where I lay, I could hear waves lashing the boat and water splashing against the floorboards of the cabin as the boat rolled. I could feel a faint breeze on my face, and somewhere from the wastelands a loon sent forth its unearthly call. We were alone in a God-forsaken world.

Our only heat during that October trip in the Bering Sea was from the little Primus stove we used for prepar-

Chris's launch, the *Evangeline*, at anchor in Kulukak Bay with George's skiff and a kayak

ing our simple meals and from the engine when the boat was moving. But for several days and nights she did not move, except for a short trip to a cove called Ten Day Creek, where we were able, at high tide, to walk on the beach.

Our meals were simple, gay occasions. The Coleman lantern hummed from its hook on the ceiling. We balanced our tin plates and coffee cups from our perches on potato crates while the boat rolled. There was much laughter and gaiety as Chris, who had grown up in a mission orphanage, told us amusing tales of the country, the people, and the wildlife. He was a pliant individual who could be one of the group, whether it was white or Eskimo.

One day, when the key to a sardine can was missing, Chris opened the can with his teeth. Another time he "shaved" his beard with a pair of clippers he had tucked away in a niche inside the boat. He was always cheerful and considerate.

Chris conversed with the boys in Yup'ik and explained to us that they understood little English. Ivan, painfully shy, avoided any contact with us. But Andrewski, comic with his stocky build and short legs that carried him with a rolling gait, always had a ready smile. He sat by the hour with his feet in reindeer boots swinging down through the hatch.

After the third day, our lunch supplies were low, and we were forced to dig into our year's provisions. We found the egg crate with thirty-two dozen wax-sealed eggs, and boiled some to eat with pilot bread dunked in black coffee. One morning, as Chris peeled off dirty, wet socks, I was sickened to see him carelessly toss them on the uncovered box of pilot bread. Still, somehow, I didn't mind the pilot bread when he bemoaned the fact that it was too late in the fall to catch spawning fish. A treat one evening was wild duck stew cooked in a battered tea kettle on the little Primus stove.

Then we moved again, this time to a cove called Protection Point, near the cape and Sterling Shoal.

"We'll get up close, and then we can sneak around the cape quick when the wind changes," Chris explained.

Once, when Chris jovially yelled down through the hatch, "We're having a hell of a time in this rough water," I shouted back, "I'm having a hell of a time, too."

I braced myself with one hand, with the other I kept the lamp from banging, and with my feet I steadied a crate of potatoes that had slipped from its niche. Spike sat on his haunches, his head low, his ears flat, and saliva drooling from his chin. Our dog was not a good sailor.

The days dragged by and the wind remained strong and raw as it blew from the sea. As time stood still and we waited for an offshore wind combined with a flood

tide, I remembered Chris saying we would have to
hurry. And I remembered Slum's telling us that Alaska
is the land of day after tomorrow, where no one hurries.
Mace, seemingly unworried, had placed his fate in
Chris's hands. He trusted the Eskimo to get him back
to Kanakanak before the Nushagak became icebound.

Evenings, as we sat huddled in the little cabin, Chris
told us tales of boats and men that had disappeared off
Cape Constantine. He said it was madness to attempt
the trip without someone who knew the reefs and without the right wind and flood tide. The old Eskimos knew
all about the cape and Sterling Shoal. They knew how
far the reef stretched out, in miles of sharp, wicked
rocks, just below the surface. A distance out from the
cape was a slight drop in the level of the rocks about a
hundred yards wide, sometimes a couple of fathoms
deep, sometimes less, depending on the tide and winds.
A boat had to pass through the reef within these hundred yards.

"Chris, how do you know where the channel is?" Ed
asked.

"Have to gauge it by distance from the cape. You
kinda get so you can tell."

Mace added ironically, "You'd never miss but once,
would you?"

It was morning, the eighth day out. Chris dropped
back in through the hatch and awakened the last
sleeper by announcing a decision.

"I think we can try it. Wind's shifted, but the water's
still plenty rough. Tide should float us in a few minutes.
She's comin' in fast."

After a hurried breakfast, Chris started the engine
and we were on our way. The water was seething. "Crab
seas," Chris called it. He was tense, alert, on guard. He
barked orders to the two boys. He was in the bow, then
in the cabin, looking at the engine, then at the wheel.
Seals bobbed all around us, sticking their heads above

the water, watching us, then disappearing. I was more frightened than I had ever been in my life.

I climbed down in the cabin. Mace whispered, "The reef is just ahead. I can tell by the way Chris is acting."

He stood in the bow with his feet spread wide to brace himself. He was holding an oar and had his eyes on the distant cape. In Yup'ik he snapped an order at Andrewski to turn the wheel. He shouted another to Ivan, and the engine slowed almost to a stop. Ed, Mace, and I scarcely breathed. In the miles of fog, how could Chris ever find a certain channel a hundred yards wide? He shoved the oar again and again into the water, sounding. I expected every minute to be jarred off my feet, to hear the bottom ripped from the boat.

Then, suddenly, Chris turned, tossed the oar on deck, and shouted orders to Ivan and Andrewski. The engine chugged at full speed, Chris grinned, and the tension was gone. Once again he was the careless, easygoing Chris. I suddenly had a wholesome respect for the man.

Much later he called me to the deck and pointed in the distance to a phantomlike island looming through the fog. It was Walrus Island, rendezvous of walrus and sea birds.

"Next spring the people of the village will go out to the island to rob the nests," he said. "Now there's a treat for you—murre eggs."

Hours later, the launch stopped rolling, and we entered the calm, sheltered waters of Kulukak Bay. Black mountains and cliffs rose from the water's edge. All was quiet except for the chugging of the boat's engine. Then it was silent, the boat dragged over sand, and the anchor dropped.

"Schoolarista," Chris announced, "your home is near the top of that hill."

4. Journey's End

With the aid of flashlights, Mace, Ed, and I made our way up the steep, muddy trail that led to the station. Ed and I knew from a plan Mace had sketched that one roof sheltered both the school and our living quarters.

Dogs yelped, seemingly by the hundreds, as we walked along the trail through the village. We heard them tug at their chains, and Mace's words spoken one evening in Kanakanak came back to me.

Don't ever underestimate the ferocity of a malamute, and never trust one."

That same evening he had told us how, at Kulukak the winter before, a dogteam had mushed down the hill above the village. The towline broke, and the dogs, free of the sled, rushed past the station, into the settlement. The vicious pack took after the one moving object in its path, a child running at play. She was torn to bits before men swinging harness chains could control the dogs. These were Kulukak dogs. I shortened Spike's leash.

Mace said, "The only sounds you'll hear from now on, other than howling winter winds, will be this malamute chorus."

He put down his traveling bag. "Wait here on the porch, and I'll go around and let you in."

Kulukak station in summer

We walked up the three steps and stood in eager anticipation. Soon the key turned in the door, and Mace welcomed us to his former bachelor quarters. A clean, closed-in smell of fresh paint welcomed us.

"Please," I thought, "don't let it be white."

Ed held the flashlight as Mace pumped and lighted the gasoline lamp. The living room had wide, low windows, and one, I knew, overlooked the bay. The walls were a soft, warm, ivory color. There was a large desk, a wall of bookshelves, a couch, and two rockers. I could see Ed in one of the chairs, listening to the radio, myself curled up on the couch, and I could almost hear the wind whistling in the stove.

The stove fascinated me. It was a tall, bulbous, potbellied affair with a fluted skirt. It was pink for want of polish, and a half-filled coal hod stood on the floor beside it.

"You'll love that funny old stove before the winter is over," Mace said. "And I'll tell you now, it'll always be pink. Polish burns off every time there's a hot fire, and that will soon be all the time."

Mace picked up a clock, wound, and set it. We waited breathlessly to hear its ticking, and the song in my heart grew loud.

Mace carried the lamp to a door that led to the bedroom. No curtains hung at the window, no bright cover was on the bed, no pictures on the walls. There was just a bed, a chair, and a chest of drawers. The floor was covered with brown battleship linoleum.

We walked back through the living room to a spotless, neat, newly painted kitchen. Soon I'd have the tea kettle singing on the black range, and I'd set the table that stood before the wide window.

Through the window I saw something bright on the hill.

"That's the reflection of the moon on a headstone," Mace said.

Chris had told me of a teacher who became "quick sick and died" in Kulukak. "Maybe heart, maybe poison," he had said. "Nobody knows."

That was many years ago. He was the first teacher to come to the village. After his death, his wife remained in Alaska, and devoted her life to helping Eskimo children. She adopted several herself and sent a blind child, whom she had found deserted in a sod house, to be educated in the States.

With quick compassion, my thoughts went to the wife left alone in this remote, isolated settlement. Making a silent promise to visit that lonely grave and to write a letter to that man's wife, I shook the shadow of its presence from my thoughts.

Mace lifted a trapdoor in the kitchen floor that opened into a shallow cellar where we would store eggs, canned milk, and anything else that should be protected from freezing. A pantry opened off the kitchen, and a door led outside to an enclosed porch where coal was stored.

Another door led through a bathroom without plumbing to a supply room with shelves that resembled a grocery store.

Then Mace, with lamp in hand, led us back through the living room into the front hall. He opened a door, and we walked into the schoolroom. It was the smallest classroom I had ever seen. One entire side was windows overlooking the bay. There was blackboard space, cupboards and shelves, stacks of books, a teacher's desk, and two sewing machines piled high with bolts of cloth and boxes of yarn. And there was another funny, pink, potbellied stove, larger than the one in the living quarters. Above the front blackboard, on a level with the bare, gray, ceiling beams, was a yellow-faced clock with a brass pendulum. Beside it dangled a frayed and knotted rope—the school bell. In one corner stood an old organ, and there were four rows of seats varying from small to large. The song in my heart grew louder.

Back in the hall, Mace opened wide cupboard doors displaying medical supplies—ointments, aspirin, cough syrup, rolls of cotton, adhesive, liniment, and bandages. He picked up a fat green book.

"This is the first-aid book—you'll use it every day," he said.

In the kitchen Mace lighted a Coleman lantern and handed it to Ed. He picked up two galvanized pails and said, "Let's get water."

"Mace, doesn't the spring freeze solid in winter?"

"Funny thing, but it never has. It'll be a slow dribble, and while the buckets fill, you'll jump up and down and stomp your feet and beat your hands together to keep warm. You'll melt snow for baths and laundry. I planned to build a shelter over the spring but never got to it. But there's lumber for it in the carpenter shack out back."

I took the lamp, and Spike and I went to the supply room to investigate on our own. There was so much food, and everything was tempting after our diet of boiled eggs and pilot bread.

I hurried to get the fire going in the range. Its roaring was a lovely sound, and at two o'clock in the morning we ate steaming oyster stew with crackers and coffee, our first meal in our new home.

At dawn we were up, eager to investigate our surroundings. From the larger window in the living room, we looked over the little blue bay, which was surrounded by brown, barren hills. A snow-covered peak rose high from the opposite shore, and a river flowed eastward. Bristol Bay was somewhere beyond the miles of tundra.

Ed searched in every direction and turned to Mace. "Not a tree in sight."

"Only willows along the creek beds," Mace replied.

Grass covered the ridge and hid the Eskimo village below us.

Mace, with a slight pensiveness in his voice, told us that even in the worst winter storms, when icy winds sweep down from the Bering Sea, the house would keep us snug and warm. He pointed out that the windows had double panes of glass and, in addition, a separate storm window. At each entrance there were double doors, one a thick, solid door and the other a heavy storm door for protection against drifting snow and strong winds.

Hurriedly, I made coffee and set it on the range while Ed dumped more coal into the firebox and stirred the coals.

"What's that at the top of the hill?" he asked.

Mace walked to the window. "That's a tripod trail marker, indicating the government-staked trail to Togiak. Looks like the framework of a tepee, doesn't it? They're placed on high places, crests of hills. This one can be seen from the bay. A traveler heads from one

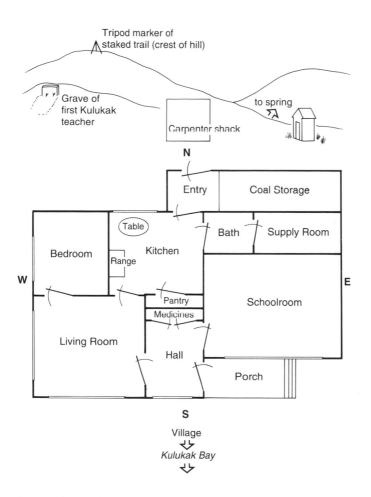

Tripod marker of staked trail (crest of hill)

Grave of first Kulukak teacher

Carpenter shack

to spring

N

Entry

Coal Storage

Table

Bath

Supply Room

Kitchen

W

Bedroom

Range

Schoolroom

Pantry

Living Room

Medicines

Hall

E

Porch

S

Village

Kulukak Bay

Station house layout

tripod to the next. Those markers are a godsend to a musher in this wilderness of rolling hills."

I suggested that we go outside. Following the trail to where it started down the hill, we saw the village. Most dwellings were sod *barabaras,* and there was a small, weatherbeaten, frame house that Mace said was the home of Peter Krause. Grass grew on the flat tops of fish caches, which were huge gray boxes built on stilts beyond the reach of dogs. Thin lines of blue smoke reached upward from the low mounds that were the dwellings. Children dressed in fur parkas laughed and shouted as they ran among the *barabaras* or through the straw-colored grass. Sled dogs lay curled in furry balls close by their stakes. One gray malamute, more restless than the others, sat on his haunches and howled mournfully and half-heartedly.

A ptarmigan, partridge of the north, called in a clipped, hollow tone, "Come here! Come here!" and darted across the tundra.

The station was a green building, low and squat, with a slightly pitched roof, a belfry and flagpole at its top. Sod was piled like bricks to window height around the structure to anchor it and tuck it snugly against winter storms. Behind the station was a little shack with the roof and a small part of the sides peeping above the sod around it. This was the carpenter shack, where tools were kept and the men gathered to build or repair sleds and kayaks. Off to the side was the outdoor plumbing.

"Do the children use the station outhouse?" I asked Mace.

"No, they do as the adults in the village—squat behind a knoll."

There were swings for the children, built of heavy timber. A trail went past them to the spring that was our water supply.

We had just returned to the warmth of the kitchen

when there was a tapping at the back door, and in walked Chris with a short, stocky man with broad shoulders and black, curly hair, neatly combed.

"In time for breakfast?" he asked.

"We're waiting for you," I answered.

"This is Peter," Mace said.

Mace and Peter were old friends. They shook hands warmly, and Mace introduced us as the new teachers. There was a reserve, a reticence, and a personal dignity to Peter Krause, not the open gregariousness we had met in Chris. I liked his firm handclasp, his steady eyes and friendly smile.

"These are good *schoolaristas,*" Chris informed him. "No sissies."

Chris and Peter had grown up together in a mission orphanage-school and, since boyhood, had been like brothers. The five of us sat down to breakfast, and the smells of ham, pancakes, and coffee filled the kitchen. Chris teased as he had on the launch and as he would in years to come.

"Coffee weak, Schoolarista. I sure can see the bottom of the cup."

He made the same remark when I made it twice as strong and boiled it twenty minutes. And he always came back for more.

Conversation turned to the work ahead. Our provisions had to be unloaded from Chris's boat, piled on the beach, and carried up the steep, muddy trail to the station. Mace's belongings had to be packed and taken down, piled separately from ours, and loaded into the boat.

"If we had some snow now," Chris said, "we could use Peter's dogs, and that'd make it easier."

We finally decided to harness the dogs anyway, so that they could help drag the radio and some of the heavier pieces up the hill. Several of the older boys in the village helped, too.

"The women and kids will be out to help. Everybody wants to see the new *schoolarista*," Chris said.

Mace turned to Peter. "Say, before I forget it," he said, "is the reindeer herd close by? They need meat at the orphanage and hoped Chris and I could bring back two or three deer."

"I'll get a couple boys off this morning to bring the herd in," Peter said. "We can butcher tomorrow morning."

The day was one of confusion and strenuous work. There were boxes and crates and people everywhere, either coming or going. As Chris had promised, all the village turned out to help. We opened each of our cases, removed the contents and piled things on the shelves in the supply room. Empty boxes were stacked in the coal shed to be used later for kindling.

The second day, while the men worked on the beach and I was alone at the station, there was a knock at the front door. A little old man in a ragged squirrelskin parka and with perhaps a dozen long black hairs on his chin smiled and greeted me with "*Cama-i.*"

"Hello," I replied.

He pushed past me, pointing to the medicine closet, smilingly assuming my consent. Opening the doors, he scanned the boxes and bottles.

"What is it you want?" I asked.

He ignored me and continued searching as I watched helplessly. At last he turned to me.

"Shit pills."

I lost no time finding the bottle labeled laxative tablets, gave him several in an envelope, and leaned against the door after he had gone. I made a mental note to teach my students another way to ask for those pills.

Later in the day, again while I was alone, there was a pounding at the front door. I answered it to find the porch full of smiling children clad in parkas.

"Hello," I said. "Won't you come in?"

They crowded into the schoolroom and huddled together near the windows. The odor of fish and of smoke from burned grass was strong and heavy.

"I'm so glad you came to see me. Won't you sit down?"

No answer. Their round little faces were expressionless, and their eyes were downcast.

"Did all of you go to school last year?"

No answer.

"My name is Mrs. Morgan. Will you each tell me your name?"

One girl giggled and glanced sidelong at the friend beside her. I turned to the tallest girl.

"Is Anecia here?"

Mace had told me that a girl named Anecia could speak some English.

"Are you Anecia?"

The girls only giggled.

"You aren't Anecia, are you?

She nodded yes.

"You are Anecia?"

"Yes, me not Anecia."

I gave up.

Thinking that some sweets would help overcome the children's shyness, I went to the supply room and filled a dish with hard candies from one of the thirty-five-pound pails we had brought. From the supply room I could hear giggling and whispering. When I offered the candy, the children stood silent and expressionless as little Buddhas. Finally, in desperation, I picked up several pieces and held them out to a child. She accepted, and I heard a faint, timid murmur "*Quyana*."

Thus I made the rounds of fourteen children. As they enjoyed the sweets and stole admiring glances at the pretty colors of one another's candies, Spike trotted into the room, and instantly all was confusion. The children shrieked in terror as Spiked raced about barking excitedly. Youngsters climbed on desks, and several ran into the hall.

A dog as a pet was unknown to the children, and they, with reason, were afraid of a loose dog. I gave Spike a piece of candy, and petted him as he crunched it. I took him to the living quarters, closed the door, and returned to the children. The day was to come when a child would tap on the door and eagerly ask, "Please, Spike he play with me?"

I asked the children if they would be glad to come to school. There were nods and more smiles, and I knew they understood more than they let on.

"There will be school in maybe three days. I'll ring the bell. Do you understand?"

I was delighted to hear one say "yes" and several say "*aang*," which I assumed meant the same thing.

As they left the building, I watched them chatting and laughing, no doubt discussing the new *schoolarista*.

How could I ever break down that shyness? How much English did they really understand, and how much could they speak? And would I ever become accustomed to the odor of fish and grass smoke?

I returned to my tasks in the supply room, happy and challenged as I anticipated the work ahead.

5. Our Work Begins

The first morning the school bell rang, youngsters—twenty-three of them—popped over the top of the knoll before the ringing stopped. They removed their parkas and hung them in the hall, and the heavy odor of grass smoke and fish filled the room. Quietly, with covert glances at one another, they found seats to their size and liking.

The boys wore plaid gingham shirts and blue jeans. The girls wore several dresses each, with those beneath showing at hems and sleeves. The patterns of the dresses matched those of the boys' shirts. Evidently, when the men shopped after the fishing or trapping season, they bought entire bolts of plaid gingham. I learned later that the girls wore several dresses because they lacked underclothing. I also learned that inside the fur boots, feet and ankles were wrapped in rags or strips of burlap from coal sacks.

The children ranged in age (I guessed because the information wasn't in the records) from five to sixteen. To my delight, there were eight teenage girls with whom I would especially enjoy working. And there was a little boy, five years old, who didn't take his eyes from

Children dressed in furs pose by the Kulukak school

me and was brave enough to smile every time I looked
his way. He was George Krause, Peter's son.

Those first days in the classroom were frustrating
and, at times, disheartening. At the end of the week I
still wondered if the children could speak any English.
Their expressionless faces remained as blank as clean
paper when I spoke to them or asked a question. If there
was any response at all, it was "*naamikika* [I don't
know]."

Gradually, I discovered that when I asked, "Will
someone close the door?" several children flew from
their seats to the entryway. Later, when I asked who
would like to do other tasks at the end of the day—take
down the flag and carefully fold it and place it in the
cupboard, or clean the blackboards and erasers, or fill
the coal hods—hands waved wildly.

If I could just get a child to talk to Ed or me, and feel

at ease doing so, I would be very happy. At night, I lay awake thinking of ways to break down that barrier of shyness. The children were more timid than any I had ever tried to teach.

Above all, never would I correct their grammar. When Nattia hesitantly whispered to me, "Please, I want headache," I gave her an aspirin tablet and several pieces of candy. Then, a few days later, with the aid of chalk and blackboard and a little printing set, I taught the children to say, "I have a headache," "I have a stomachache," "I am sick."

Whenever a child spoke to me, I gave my full attention, because having to repeat the message made him or her become silent and shy. My delight was unbounded one afternoon soon after school started, when I walked through the village and George caught up and walked along with me. Because I wanted him to be at ease, I only smiled and said, "Hello." He was silent, and then, mustering his courage, asked, "How you was?"

It was weeks before some of the children ever spoke a word to me other than *naamikika*. Ed said that their reserve would melt as they got to know us, and he suggested having parties for them in the schoolroom.

At first they sat and watched as Ed and I struggled to entertain them at the parties. We played the half-dozen scratchy records we had, and I did my best pumping the wheezy organ. Gradually, we got them into the games. We had taffy pulls in the kitchen, went on hikes, and played games in which they had to speak English. Children who thanked me with "*quyana*" won only a smile from me, while those who said "thank you" were praised. And they were anxious to earn the *schoolarista*'s favor.

The reading textbooks were inadequate, so with the little printing set and tagboard we made our own stories.

Stephan killed a seal.
It was a big spotted seal.
Stephan's mother skinned it.
She will make fur boots for Stephan.

Wassilia trapped a red fox.
He will take it to the trading post.

Chunook has a new parka.
Her mother and Anecia made it for her.

The reindeer herd is near the village.
We like to eat reindeer meat.

Stephan illustrated his story by drawing a seal and his new fur boots. Chunook made a picture of her parka, and Michael sketched beautiful reindeer. Around the room I fastened labels to objects, such as chair, desk, clock, door, window.

Then one day, as I noticed a stack of little notebooks in the cupboard, I thought of diaries. This was the best idea of all because the children became keenly interested in them. And I liked them, too, for as time went on, the children's statements gave me insights into their lives and interests outside the classroom. Sometimes they wrote about things they found difficult or were hesitant to say. One might write, "On my leg is bad hurt," and that would bring to light a tender, throbbing boil. Or perhaps "I am little bit stomachache." Many of the statements were precious bits of newly acquired English. Ocalena, desiring to say that baby Willie was always cheerful, wrote, "Willie, he is happying all the time."

The students sometimes asked Anecia how to write the English words they wanted to tell me. Often they used their diaries to make requests, such as, "Please, I

Stephan, Charlie, and Michael

have soap for I wash my face." Or they would thank me
for some little gift or kindness, such as, "Mrs. Morgan
help me make cap. I am just glad."

In the back pages of the notebooks they copied the
words of songs we had learned. They drew stick figures
and labeled the parts of the body. They were wonderful
students, and they watched my every movement. Morn-
ings they were huddled on the porch, eagerly waiting

to come in. Usually all twenty-three were there, and I had no need to pull the rope that rang the bell on the roof.

Friday evenings became the children's night, and everyone helped move the rows of desks to the side of the schoolroom. They gathered to play games, listen to our radio, and dance to the records scratched out by the old phonograph.

Ed remarked one evening as he returned from starting a slow fire in the school stove an hour before party time, "There are heads peering over the snowbank already."

No one would be in sight when he walked into the room with the humming Coleman lamp at seven o'clock to pull the bell rope. The peals floated clearly over the village, far out on the waters of the bay, and over the silent tundra. Moments later, the children came scampering up the porch steps.

During the day there had been soft whispers, muffled giggles, and eyes sparkling with anticipation. The four older boys—Andrewski, Ivan, Madfy, and Koopik—left their reindeer herds to return to the village for the Friday evening parties.

At first the children were too shy to dance. Ed and I danced together, then he danced with Anecia and asked the other girls to dance with him while I asked the boys to dance with me. During our second part, Ed was standing by the door between dances when little Petusa, a first grader, walked over and stood before him, her fingers nervously twisting her skirt.

"Please to dance."

That started something with the three first-grade girls that followed at every party. Ed picked up Petusa and, to her delight, danced with her in his arms.

Though the parties had started for the school children, the adults soon became involved as well. While we played games one evening, Ed's eyes caught shadows

Children of Kulukak

on the snowbanks outside. Huddled in their parkas, snow swirling around them, several people stood peering through the windows, vicariously enjoying the merriment inside. We immediately invited them in, and from that time on both grown-ups and children were welcome. The adults were an interested audience, but seldom participated in the fun.

The villagers found fun in everything, sometimes at our expense. At the first party, Ed was desperately in need of a haircut. Because Mace had cut the children's hair, they expected me to do likewise. My first attempts had not been very satisfactory, and I was grateful that a couple of weeks would erase my mistakes. After school, George, Stephan, and Michael each took his turn, perched happily on the organ stool with a cape I had fashioned from a flour sack tied around his neck while I worked with scissors and clippers. After seeing my first attempts, Ed decided to let his hair grow. That evening, at the back of the room, mischievous little Gus mocked Ed's shaggy head by pulling at his own hair on either side of his forehead and wickedly whispering, Mr. Morgan."

Glancing at Ed across the room, I sent the message "Serves you right."

That night, after the party, he sat stiffly on the organ stool, clutching my blue apron around his neck with one hand and my dressing table mirror in the other while I clipped and snipped.

Our parties ended with treats—colored popcorn balls, candy and peanuts, or, perhaps, cookies and hot chocolate. Anecia and the older girls proudly helped prepare and serve the treats. At evening's end, the people left with happy smiles and the words *"quyana, schoolaristas."*

But the classroom and the children did not have my undivided attention those first days and weeks. Scrubbing clothes on a washboard was a new experience for me. I learned that a frozen garment was best removed gently from the clothesline and not folded. I showed Ed his favorite shirt, with a hole where every fold had been.

Remembering the bread I had taken for granted Outside, I struggled with the brief recipe Ted had scribbled on an envelope. I turned the handle of the aluminum bread mixer as she said I should, and I carefully tucked a blanket around the dough at night so it would rise. The following day, I put it in the oven, and when the brown and crusty finished product came out, the house was filled with a delicious aroma. Ed always made a pot of coffee and cut off a heel of the warm bread, covered it with butter and brown sugar, and told me that when we were back Outside I must continue to bake bread.

While my work was inside, Ed's was outdoors. One morning he came into the kitchen and called to me.

"Come see the reindeer."

I tied my robe around me and hurried to the window. Near the crest of the snow-covered hill, under the clear blue skies of early morning, were the reindeer, the first I had seen. A big bull, on the fringe of the herd, pawed the snow seeking a morsel of moss. He was a handsome animal. His hindquarters were dark in color, his shoulders heavy with a shaggy white ruff, and his head carried a set of wide antlers. The herd moved constantly in search of lichens, and as they raised their heads to listen, graceful antlers were outlined against the sky.

"I feel I should turn the page and read the greeting inside," I said. "But why are they here? Peter said the dogs kept them away from the village."

"The people need fresh meat, and the closer to the village they butcher the less distance they have to carry the meat," Ed replied. "Peter is to kill only the white does. They're to be eliminated from the breeding herd."

Ed was intent on the deer.

"If we were outside now, we could hear antlers hit against antlers. Every deer, male and female, has antlers."

But I was disappointed. I thought of the slender, graceful deer that held their heads high in illustrations of Santa's sleigh. These animals were sturdy of build, and they held their heads no higher than their bodies. Ed poured a cup of coffee and brought it to where I stood at the window.

"This is only a fraction of the herd," he said. "A thousand of them are scattered over the tundra. It will take a long time to gather them together. Late next summer

Reindeer from the Kulukak herd

they'll have to be counted, marked, and the males cas-
trated."

Ed spent hours at the desk studying the range rules,
the records, and the journals on handling reindeer. It
was a complicated business. Eskimos traditionally were
hunters, not herders. They enjoyed the meat, and made
good use of the hides, but they turned to the reindeer
only when other game was scarce. The deer roamed the
tundra, flocked together like sheep, grazing on moss,
grass, lichens, and willows. They were herded by boys
who, through apprenticeship, eventually acquired
herds of their own. Ed found the deer to be gentle and
extremely timid. Mace said that their intelligence was
close to that of horses.

While working on reports one evening, Ed found that
Peter Krause owned most of the Kulukak herd. Among

other owners' names listed were Rose Nose and Red Nose's Sister, written in parentheses below names such as Aigogiyuwak, Chakookwylnok, and Gusuklaulra. My amusement was short-lived, however, because of a notation written at the bottom of the page by a former teacher: "We received no mail from the time we arrived here in September until a team came through from Nushagak the following March 13."

The reindeer work, I knew, was a constant source of concern to Ed. Peter resented outside interference and was uncooperative. After one long day on the tundra, Ed was working at the desk when Peter knocked at the door.

"Just hung half a deer on the cross beam of the swings for you," he said.

"But we haven't used all of that last quarter," Ed replied.

"I threw it to the dogs."

A steak or roast had been a rare luxury for us the winter before, and we could not help being thrifty with meat. We, like the Eskimos, enjoyed the reindeer meat. I made rich broths and soups, we had delicious steaks and roasts, and, when ground together with ham, reindeer meat made a tasty loaf or patties.

From the tallow we made soap for the children's use at school and for the women's housekeeping. The soap was made by rendering the fat, slowly adding a mixture of lye and water to the melted tallow, and stirring for a long time. Then it was emptied into a flat wooden mold where, after a couple of days, it was cut into bars. After aging for two weeks, it was ready for use.

Dispensing medicine and giving medical aid took much of Ed's time and attention. The thick green book, dog-eared from use, surely had been written for inexperienced young teachers who were trying to help sick or injured Eskimos. The nearest doctor and hospital were at Kanakanak. In summer that meant a trip around the cape, and in winter a two-day dogsled journey. The Eskimos were extremely reluctant to go to the doctor or the hospital—it was where one went to die.

It seemed that someone always had a boil or boils. Old Anuska had a horrid boil on her arm, and Ed cared for it by the book. Anuska was not very cooperative, and she watched Ed suspiciously as he dressed the sore. Days later she returned, pulled off her parka, her skirts tucked tightly between her knees, and held out her arm triumphantly. The angry redness and swelling, and the sterile dressing, were gone. Before we could gleam with pride at such wondrous results, we saw that over the open sore was a patch of squirrelskin.

One day I answered the door to find the old man in the ragged parka who had come for laxative tablets soon after our arrival. He was Wassilia Aigogiyuwak. He smilingly requested *suungcautet* (medicine). I opened the medicine cabinet and reached for the brown bottle before he could ask for it. But he shook his head. With a pained expression, he repeated something over and over in Yup'ik. He put his hand on his back and hobbled around, and then, in seeming agony, straightened up.

"Aspirin?" I held up the bottle.

He shook his head *"Non,"* and again hobbled about with his hands on his back.

"Liniment, Wassilia?"

"Aang! Aang!" He nodded his head, all smiles. *"Quyana,* Schoolarista."

Later in the winter, Charlie, an older boy whose merry eyes always had a life-is-wonderful look, came in from the reindeer camp. On his neck, under a raw sore, was a large, hard swelling.

"Charlie," I said, "this should have been taken care of long ago. You can't go back out with the deer till it's healed."

This was something that wasn't covered in the green

Charlie, in his mink parka, in front of a *barabara*. Fish caches are in the background.

book, and Ed was at a loss as to how to treat it. Charlie stood smiling while Ed taped thick layers of gauze over the ugly, draining sore.

"Charlie, you'll have to go to Kanakanak and see the doctor," Ed said. "Come up tonight and let me put a clean dressing on and give you a letter for the doctor. He'll have your neck all well soon."

Resignedly, but still smiling, Charlie nodded.

"The weather's good for traveling," Ed remarked. "If you leave early and travel alone, you might make it over in one day."

Three days later we saw Charlie and his team return. Ed hoped he would have instructions from the doctor with him and, possibly, if a mail plane had been into Dillingham, some letters for us.

"Hello, Charlie," Ed smiled. "Have a good trip?"

"*Aang.*"

"See the doctor?"

"*Aang.*"

Ed pulled back Charlie's parka hood to look at his neck. The sore was without dressing, was draining profusely, and was so swollen Charlie could not hold his head straight.

"Charlie," Ed said sternly, "did you see the doctor?"

"*Aang.*"

"Did you go to his office at the hospital?"

"*Aang.*"

"Did you give him my letter, and did he look at your neck?"

"*Aang.*" Charlie shrugged his shoulders. "But it do no good."

Ed helped Charlie stake out his dogs and then had him come up to the station. Carefully, Ed cleaned the horrible sore, and in the days that followed Charlie spent many hours by the range in our kitchen while Ed kept hot compresses on his neck. Gradually the draining stopped, the swelling subsided, and the sore began to heal.

About this time a team came through Kulukak and dropped off our mail. In a bold scrawl, in the doctor's handwriting, was a note demanding, "Where in hell did your Charlie go? I left him in my office to go across the hall for dressing. When I came back, he was gone. Nobody here has seen him since."

Another trying case was that of Shaky Andrew, who suffered from what we supposed was a form of palsy. He trembled constantly and walked bent forward. He was young and had an attractive, industrious wife named Olia, who lovingly and tenderly cared for him. Anecia summed up his case for us.

"Shaky Andrew no can hunt, no can fish," she said. "He no can chew hard food, no dry fish. Olia all the time cook soft foods for Andrew. Andrew no can hold anythings. Olia feed him."

We learned that Shaky Andrew and Olia were held in high regard by the entire village. Neither spoke English, but language wasn't necessary to endear them to us.

One day I sent Andrew a kettle of reindeer soup, and Anecia returned, saying, "Andrew glad. Say soup good. Olia pleased." She was pulling off her parka when we heard someone at the door. There stood Olia, holding out to me a pan of smelts, stiffly frozen. She had caught them that morning in the river channel, and this was her way of thanking me. Andrew and Olia were proud, hurrying to return any gift or favor. While we were at Kulukak, I never took bread from the oven or soup from the kettle without thinking of Shaky Andrew. We came to know his knock on the station door and his smile of satisfaction and friendship as he gave us fish or ptarmigan caught by Olia. Once, during fox season, Andrew came into the kitchen and held out a paper for me to take. Unwrapping it, I found a five-dollar bill, neatly folded.

"Oh, no, Andrew, I can't take this," I said.

Suddenly the expression of happiness faded from his face, and a look of hurt came into his eyes.

"You want me to have it?" I asked lamely.

He was pleased when I put the money in my apron pocket.

"*Aang,* Schoolarista, *aang.*"

Satisfied, he turned and shuffled out the door. Tears came to my eyes as I looked at Ed and thought of how Olia had either trapped a fox or traded for that five dollars.

I was never certain how much English Andrew understood. One day he came to the station with little George to get some aspirin for Olia. As the two stood in the hall, I noticed them intently listening to the radio, so I invited them in. Andrew, without a word from George, went immediately to the living room and sat on the couch.

Teacherlike, but not hostesslike, I said to my little first grader, "George, what about boys and their caps in the house?" Sheepishly, George pulled off his fur cap. Instantly, Andrew muttered something to George, and the boy jumped up and pulled back Andrew's parka hood. I smiled my approval, but inwardly I was ashamed and taken aback that Andrew had understood me.

Another person at Kulukak, Old Nattia, especially won our sympathy and affection. Nattia seemed to belong nowhere, but Big Wassilia fed and sheltered her. I first met her when I answered a tapping at the back door and found her sitting on the snow-covered stoop. She was wearing a faded and mended red sweater and a bandana tied over her head. The skirts of her checkered gingham dress were wet and dirty around her sealskin boots. Annie, a schoolgirl, stood nearby.

"Who is she, Annie?"

"Old Nattia. Legs bad. No walk."

Annie explained that Nattia had dragged herself through the wet snow, up the hill to the station.

"Tell her I'd like her to come in. And you come, too, Annie," I said.

Nattia dragged herself through the entry into the kitchen, where she sat on the floor near the stove. From the folds of her clothing, she produced two small baskets made of beach grass, and held them out to me.

"She want soap and tea," Annie said.

I accepted the baskets as a gift because Old Nattia would have been deeply hurt if I had refused them. She was all smiles when I handed her the soap and tea.

"Annie," I said, "ask her if she has ever let the doctor look at her legs."

Annie spoke to the woman in Yup'ik, then turned to me.

"She go to doctor a long time ago. Two doctors. Got no better. Awful hurt sometimes."

I knelt beside Nattia and touched her sodden skirts, then turned to Annie.

"Tell her never, never, to let her legs get wet and cold like this. It's very bad for them. Makes them hurt more. Tell her not to come up here like this, but to send someone for me, and I will come see her."

I supposed it would not help much, but I gave her aspirin, liniment, and a hot water bottle and told Annie to show her how to use them. Annie then went for help, and Nattia rode by dogsled back to Big Wassilia's house.

6. Anecia

Among our closest friends was Anecia, who helped in the schoolroom and often served as an interpreter. She had come to introduce herself soon after our arrival. A young Eskimo woman, perhaps sixteen years old, she had worn a fur parka, and a black bandana framed her face as she stood at our door.

"I am Anecia," she said softly.

"I'm so happy to see you," I replied. "Do come in. Peter said you were visiting across the harbor."

"Today I come back."

I stood in the doorway to the living room as she removed the most beautiful parka I was to see during my years in Alaska. It was mink, trimmed with white fur and tassels of red yarn. She hung it on one of the hooks provided for the school children. She did not smile, but looked directly at me and I felt her friendliness. She was small, and her skin was light, almost pale. Her short, black hair was straight and shiny clean. I learned later that her plaid gingham dress, faded red sweater, heavy ribbed black stockings, and brown shoes several sizes too large were her best clothes.

Mace had told us something of Anecia's life. She was one of the older children of a large family. Her father, an industrious man who had a trace of Russian blood, was once the chief herder of the Kulukak reindeer, but now was in extremely poor health. Anecia's mother was a tireless worker who snared ptarmigan, fished for smelt through the river ice, prepared hides for boots and parkas, gathered willow twigs from along the creeks, and carried the bundles home on her back. Anecia, when she was about thirteen, had lived with a white family, former teachers at Kulukak. She quickly adapted herself to a new way of life, learning to speak English and to keep house.

When the teachers left the village, Anecia returned to her parents' *barabara* and, after a year, she married a young man from Togiak. Her husband was injured in a shooting accident and was recovering in the Kanakanak hospital when he died in a scarlet fever epidemic that swept through Bristol Bay. He was buried in Kanakanak, and Anecia, grieving deeply, returned to her family in Kulukak. There she was highly respected and much sought after because she was attractive and industrious. She knit caps and mittens, and helped with most of the sewing done in the settlement.

She sat in the rocking chair by the stove, speaking little. I thought perhaps she was shy, but it was not the same bashfulness I had seen in the children who kept their eyes downcast. Anecia's serious eyes were direct, but she was pensive and wistful.

"Anecia, would you like to help me pop corn?" I asked.

For the first time, she smiled. She was eager to help. Later, when she said she had to leave, Ed and I walked her to the village.

"I like to come to school?" she said. It was a question.

"I'd like very much to have you," I replied.

From then on, I found her invaluable as an interpreter. She helped not only with the children who spoke no English, but also with adults who came for medicine or other aid. She spent many evenings at the station

Anecia in her mink
parka.

listening to the radio, or looking at our few books and
sometimes asking questions. When Ed was out of the
house, she talked to me of the country and of her people's
customs. When Ed came into the room, however, she
retreated behind a book.

One evening, Ed and Alexie, a middle-aged man of
mixed ancestry visiting the village, came in from re-
pairing a sled in the carpenter shack. The four of us
listened to the news broadcast, and Anecia became

tense, scarcely raising her eyes from her clasped hands. Alexie picked up his cap and, glancing at her, asked, "You go now?"

Terror showed on her face. She jumped to her feet and, standing behind the chair, gripped its back so tightly her knuckles were white.

"No," she shouted. "I not go now."

Alexie's face flushed with anger, and he spoke sharply to her in Yup'ik. Anecia neither moved nor answered. He shrugged his shoulders and left. Ed went with him.

While I prepared bread dough in the kitchen and Ed returned to the living room, Anecia stood quietly by, uneasily rubbing her palms together. Soon she went to the hall and returned, wearing her parka.

"Now I go."

She stood hesitant before the door, then opened it and looked fearfully about her.

"Anecia are you afraid of something?" I asked. "Come back in. What's troubling you?"

"Please," she said. "I sleep here tonight?"

She hung up her parka but would say nothing. That night she wore a pair of my pajamas and tucked herself into bed on the living room couch. We knew she was deeply grateful for the protection we had given her.

As the weeks passed and Ed was busy with his work, sometimes away for days at a time with the reindeer, Anecia came often to the station, and I grew increasingly fond of her. She chatted and laughed happily while sewing or knitting or helping me with my work. Still, however, a shadow hung over her happiness, and she explained nothing.

Then Koopcha, Alexie's son, stopped over in Kulukak. That evening he came to the school party very drunk from a yeasty Eskimo brew called *piivaq*. Going straight to Anecia, he asked her to dance, and she refused. Ed had made it known that no one was to come near the station if he had been drinking, and more than once he had escorted a drunken villager down the trail to his *barabara.*

Koopcha sat sullen, and soon left. Again Anecia asked if she could spend the night at the station. The following morning, an angry Alexie came in while Ed, Anecia, and I were having breakfast. He spoke angrily to Anecia then turned to Ed.

"She wouldn't dance with Koopcha."

Ed tried to pass it off lightly. "Lady can dance with whomever she pleases, Alexie."

"Anecia belongs in the village. She thinks she's too good for Koopcha."

"Koopcha should not have come here drunk," Ed said.

Soon Alexie left, and Anecia finally confided in us.

"I afraid of Alexie," she said. "For a long time he say I marry Koopcha. Please, I not want to."

She explained that village teachers often had forced couples to marry and that she was afraid Alexie would ask me to arrange her marriage to Koopcha.

A few evenings later, Anecia's father came to the station. He had been drinking, and I sat with Ed in the living room while father and daughter spoke in the kitchen.

"*Qang'a* [no]*! Qang'a!* she cried, then burst into the living room and put her arms around me. "My father say Alexie tell him I have to marry Koopcha."

"You don't have to marry Koopcha," Ed replied.

He went into the kitchen, but Anecia's father had gone. Later her father returned to the door and told Anecia that Alexie wanted to see her. She was terrified.

Ed told Anecia, "Tell him I said if Alexie wants to see you, for him to come here."

Her father left, and shortly her mother appeared, wringing her hands and talking excitedly.

"She say Alexie beat her if she not bring me back," Anecia told us. "My parents much afraid."

"Get your parka," Ed said. "I'll go with you."

When he returned later with Anecia, he was more angry than I had ever seen him. They had entered Anccia's parents' *barabara* to find Alexie and Koopcha there, Alexie at the *piivaq* barrel.

"Koopcha wants to marry her," Alexie said. "She's put him off long enough. She has to marry Koopcha."

Anecia then gathered her courage and screamed at Alexie, "I won't marry Koopcha! I hate him! I won't marry anybody!"

Alexie pulled himself up from the bunk on which he had been sitting and, reeling and staggering, lunged at Ed. Ed shoved him back on the bunk and told Anecia's parents that they could come to the station if they were afraid of Alexie and Koopcha.

The next day, a meek and humble Alexie came to the station and acted as if nothing had happened to mar the usual fellowship. We made no reference to the previous evening, but decided that Anecia would live with us for a while.

For the next week, her terrified shrieks tore through the night. Ed and I sprang from our beds and dashed to the living room. Her eyes were wide with fear.

"*Carayak* [spirit] in here!" she cried.

"Anecia, you were dreaming. The doors are locked. How could it get in?" I said.

"*Naamikika, carayaks* just come in."

She stood wringing her hands. "Schoolarista, *carayak* touch me."

My scalp tingled. Turning the wick of the lamp higher, I began to straighten Anecia's bedding. Ed picked up the flashlight.

"Anecia, he said, "we'll search the house. Then will you feel better?"

She nodded, then said, "But I be glad if you leave on light."

Anecia, looking demure bundled in the afghan, fur slippers, and nightgown, timidly followed Ed into the hall. Spike trotted along.

I heard Ed say, "Try the outside door, Anecia. Locked, isn't it?"

As they returned to the living room, Ed's expression said as clearly as words, "Of all the damned nonsense."

Anecia reluctantly slipped off the afghan and slippers. Ed leaned against the desk and contemplated Spike, who stood beside the couch, tail wagging. She touched the dog's cold little nose and then grinned sheepishly at Ed and me. As she crawled back into bed, I smoothed the afghan over her. Ed turned the lamp low.

"You don't need the light now, do you Anecia?" he said.

"Yes."

"Yes?"

"Yes, I don't need any light now."

But our experience with spirits was not at an end. Another time Anecia came running into the kitchen, shouting, "Schoolarista! Come quick! *Carayak* in the sewing machine. He in drawer. Make awful noise."

Sure enough, when I investigated, sounds came from the drawer. Ed recently had caught two mice in the cellar, but we had seen none upstairs. I moved closer to the machine. As I did so, Spike jumped and darted toward me. The noise increased. I opened the drawer and suddenly a spool of black thread began to jump. Anecia watched, spellbound. I grabbed the thread and pulled, and as I did, the spool leaped even more. The other end was tangled around Spike's foot, and when he moved, the spool bounced.

"Anecia, I said, "there's your *carayak*."

As I left the room, she said, apologetically, "Schoolarista, sometimes *carayaks* hide in places."

As time slipped by, Anecia fit more and more into our home, and we became increasingly fond of her. She talked of the ways of her people, and it was clear she was entirely loyal to them. And, as she proved at one of our Friday evening gatherings, she was loyal to us as well.

While dressing for the party, I succumbed to nostalgia for other Friday evenings Ed and I had known at college, and unpacked my favorite dress from its garment bag and the high heeled pumps that had been in their box since we left Washington. When I emerged from the bedroom, Ed's admiring glances and Anecia's "You beautiful white lady" soared my spirits.

Shortly after the bell rang, the young reindeer herders arrived. Andrewski, who had been a source of quiet amusement to Ed and me since our boat trip from Kanakanak, appeared with hair slicked back and shirt collar turned up at a rakish angle. He danced with abandon in fur boots, keeping perfect time with the music. After dancing with Anecia, he dropped into a chair, and, as I walked across the room, he made a loud remark in Yup'ik. All eyes followed me with giggles. Suddenly, quiet Anecia jumped from her chair and shouted angrily across the room at Andrewski. He then became the uncomfortable object of amusement.

"Whatever it is, Andrewski and I seem to have it in common," I remarked to Ed.

After the party, I asked Anecia about it. She was reluctant to answer, but I persisted. Carefully choosing her words and shaking her head, she said, "That Andrewskii. Sometimes not good boy. Makes fun of peoples."

"Did he make fun of me?"

"*Aang*. All the time he sees women in fur boots, not like you wear tonight. He tell everybody, 'Schoolarista have legs skinny like a crane's.' "

"And what did you say to him?"

"I say, 'Andrewski, shut up! You have legs short and bowed like fish duck's.' "

One afternoon Anecia and I stood on the edge of the bluff above the frozen bay. I saw no sign of life or movement, not even a bird, in the snow-blanketed world. Anecia pointed to the icy river that wound its way from the harbor into the hills.

"See, womans gets smelts now," she said.

Just above the mouth of the river, there were a number of minute black specks, each of which was a woman. We climbed down the trail and crossed the ice of the bay. The bay was not as level as it appeared from above. It held ridges, hummocks, and deep, narrow cracks an inch wide and of limitless length. The ice crunched under the soles of our mukluks. We heard a sharp, brittle snap, and then another long, deep crack appeared. Uneasily, I hurried on until Anecia explained that the rising and falling of the tide under the ice cause it to crack, and that the ice near the shore was at least five feet thick.

We followed in the trail of a dogsled. The thought came to me that Alaska was beautiful but rugged— beautiful with its snow, rivers, and mountains, but rugged in its isolation, cold, storms, strong winds, and tides. As we drew near to the women, they waved and called a welcoming *"Cama-i, cama-i."* Each sat before a hole of about ten inches in diameter, her feet under her parka. In mittened hands, she held a pole not more than two feet long, to which was attached a string of perhaps three feet. At the end of the line was a small, carved ivory fish with a hook attached. The jerking pole caused the line to bob up and down in the water, and every fourth or fifth jerk brought up a smelt.

Another woman joined the group, picked up her walrus-bone spear, and drove it into the ice. She worked until water bubbled up, then bailed the floating ice

Anecia, Spike and I (left) on the island in Kulukak Bay.

Barabara in the making. Photo on left shows the bare framework, and photo on right shows the framework covered with sod.

chips from the hole. There the ice was perhaps a foot thick. She seated herself and arranged her parka over her folded legs. Then she unwound her line, dropped the little ivory fish into the hole, and jerked her line. It wasn't long before smelts were scattered about her on the ice. The women fished and chatted until the tide went out, then gathered up the frozen fish and returned to the village.

I wasn't yet acquainted with all the village residents and did not know which *barabara* each lived in. One hut stood apart from the others, near the edge of the bluff, and as Anecia and I made our way back to the station, I asked her who lived there.

"Nobody," she said. "That *qasgiq*."

"What's that?"

"Men's house. Take sweat baths. Only mens go inside."

The following summer, when the villagers were at their fish camp and Ed and I were alone at Kulukak, he took me inside the *qasgiq*. Like the other *barabaras,* it had a low outer door, a narrow, long, low tunnel, an inner door, and a large room with a dome-shaped ceiling. A yellowed walrus-gut window at the top let in scattered light. Two tiers of bunks lined the sides and end of the room. In the center a pit, four feet in diameter, was filled with large rocks. These the men heated until red and doused with water to make steam for sweat baths.

Long ago, before contact with outsiders, village life had centered around the *qasgiq*. The older boys and old men lived in the dwelling, and only young boys and married men lived in huts and were part of the family circle. When a boy was old enough to hunt and trap fox, mink, otter, muskrat, ermine, and beaver; when he outgrew women's work of snaring ptarmigan, fetching wood, hunting in the marshes for duck and gull eggs; when he could handle a dogteam and kayak; when he played a man's part in sailing open seas; and when he brought home his first seal, then he was no longer in need of a mother's protection. He was ready to make the *qasgiq* his abode.

There the older men told him the tricks of trapping the fox, and the artifice of hunting the walrus. They taught him to build a kayak, bending the willow ribs by chewing them soft. He learned to carve ivory for his spears and to lay a trapline. And he was warned to leave the claws of the animal on the carcass, never on the pelt, so the spirit would be content and pacified and not follow him. He learned to spear salmon, to make his way in a kayak across a river of ice floes, perhaps turning over, but always reaching the opposite shore. He learned to build a sled, digging curved roots, two alike, to serve as runners.

When people from the Outside came, the old ways changed. The once exalted *qasgiq* became simply a sweat-bath house. The village was still organized, still a clan, and at the *qasgiq,* the men still chose their *tyone* (chief), the one whose judgment they pledged themselves to respect and follow.

7. The Children

"Please, Schoolarista, you help me make dress? I have cloth."

Sophia stood in the doorway, her round face framed in a red cotton bandana and her large brown eyes pleading. Flakes of snow clung to her scarf, to the shoulders of her parka, and to the folds of gingham she held in her arms.

School had been in session only a short time, and I had not yet organized the sewing class, although I wanted each girl to make several articles of flannel underclothing. Sophia was so eager and excited to make a dress that I didn't have the heart to suggest that she wait a month or so till we got to it in the classroom. She wanted her dress right then.

"My father come from Nushagak," she said. "Bring me cloth. I be glad."

Placing her precious cloth on the couch, she returned to the hall and pulled off her parka. The dress she had on was also plaid gingham, homely in its colors and pattern. She had made it herself, a T-shaped garment with a hole cut for the neck and extensions for sleeves. It was full and straight, with a cord tied about the hips.

"What kind of dress do you want to make, Sophia? We'll have to know before we start."

66

She shrugged, then eyed the dress she was wearing. As I looked at it, I, too, decided that this time Sophia should have something as pretty as we could make it.

"Sophia," I said, "do you like the green dress I wear when I'm working in the living quarters?"

Her face lighted up. "Yes, Schoolarista."

She was ecstatic as she wriggled into the green dress and went to the bathroom to shyly admire herself in the mirror.

"This most beautiful dress."

I explained that we had to use a pattern to make a dress. Since there was no store in which to buy a paper pattern, we could rip the seams of my dress, take it apart, press it, and cut a pattern from it. Then we would put that paper pattern on Sophia's cloth, and cut out her dress.

"Would you like to do that?" I asked.

She nodded enthusiastically.

Sophia's dress was not yet complete when, in the other girls' diaries, there appeared statements such as, "Evon go to Nushagak. Maybe bring me cloth. Please, I bring it up here and make dress like Sophia dress."

The day Sophia finished her dress, she carefully pressed it with the old sadiron that had been heated on top of the stove, slipped it on a hanger, and hung it by the blackboard at the front of the room. The other girls stood about admiring it as Sophia stepped up to straighten a sleeve. She sat down, but a minute later was up again adjusting the collar. She sat at a desk, chin cupped in hand, staring worshipfully at her dress.

"Schoolarista, please I put on my dress?" she said finally.

I nodded, and a few minutes later she shyly but proudly emerged from the bedroom, smoothing the skirt with trembling fingers.

"It's beautiful," she said. "I looked in mirror."

But more important than the new dress she wore

was the rapt expression on her face. At that moment, I achieved the ultimate in joy and gratification as a teacher. The girls chattered excitedly in Yup'ik, and Sophia's face told me they were saying nice things about her dress.

Before Sophia had ripped apart my green dress, I had written an urgent plea to my family for colored tape, bright edgings, and pretty buttons. It might be weeks before a dogteam traveled to Nushagak with my letter and months more before a package could reach us, but what a delight it would be when it did arrive.

Ocalena, who had no one to bring her fabric, became the proud owner of my disassembled dress, and joyfully put the pieces together again. So, in our sewing class, instead of working up to the making of a dress, we started with dresses and worked down to more simple garments.

Not one of the girls possessed a slip, and outing flannel made warmer underclothes than did an extra cotton dress. They made shirts with short sleeves and panties with calf-length legs. Lucy gave me an idea for material for panties. Running outside one day for afternoon recess, she slipped on the icy porch and her skirts flew up. Across her little posterior, in bold blue letters, blazed the words "Sperry's Drifted Snow." In the supply room I found a box of empty flour sacks. Bleached and laundered, they made excellent material for underclothing.

None of the girls had a western-style coat. In the winter they wore parkas, and in summer, if they were lucky, cardigan sweaters. Nattia, a little girl whose poverty-striken family had recently moved to Kulukak, came to school in a man's ragged khaki army coat. The garment reached below the child's knees, and she was almost lost in the broad shoulders. The frayed cuffs were turned up to allow her hands to be free from the long sleeves.

We made jackets for the girls from bolts of blue denim,

Ocalena modeling the dress, knitted cap, and blue denim jacket she made in the classroom

and had knit caps and mittens from yarn. Trying out a new pattern I cut for the girls to use, I made a pair of denim mittens and gave them to George. He was so delighted, he refused to take them off even in school. Once, when Ed sent him to take a note to his father, he

The schoolgirls in their new winter parkas

left hurriedly wearing his mittens but without his parka or cap.

When each girl completed her jacket, knitted cap, and mittens, Ed took a picture of her proudly wearing her new outfit.

Eskimo mittens, made from fur or sealskin, were ill-fitting. The general shape was that of a mitten with a hole cut in the vicinity of the thumb. Into that hole was sewed a puckered cylinder at right angles. Taking an old canvas glove, we disregarded the fingers and made a pattern. Each girl then made her own copy of the pattern for future use.

After school the girls sat at the library table, sewing

and chatting. Sometimes they made shirts for little brothers, garments for little sisters, or dresses for the women of the village. Sometimes a girl would ask if she could iron her dress after washing it, taking pride in making it look new. Up to this time, they had never used irons. Each girl had her own patterns, neatly folded and labeled, and tucked with her treasures in a box or sack in a corner of the humble hut in which her family lived.

During the summer, the director at Kanakanak sent a box of footwear to be distributed among needy children. Annie, one of the older girls, had never owned a pair of shoes or stockings, and had worn instead only cleaned coal sacks cut into strips and bound around her feet. Some of the people folded a layer of dry beach grass over their toes, tying it in place. This traditional footwear kept them warm and dry. The Eskimos had never seen manufactured shoes, and when I put the box from Kanakanak in the schoolroom, Annie stared longingly at the boys' oxford shoes.

"I like to have shoes like that," she said.

"They're small sizes, Annie," I said, "but if there's a pair that fits, you may have them."

She found the biggest pair, but they were still too small, and I knew they would hurt her feet. But when she eagerly insisted, "They not too small," I didn't have the heart to refuse her. She walked off with them, smiling happily, unable to take her eyes from her feet.

Life was never dull in the classroom, and I enjoyed every minute I spent with the children. Though a few times in Kulukak I questioned the wisdom of William Seward's squandering two cents an acre for Alaska in 1867, I never had those doubts while in the classroom. There were times, however, when my resolve was tested, such as one day not long after our arrival, when I made a disturbing discovery. The first graders were gathered around the library table for reading class, listening intently to every word I said. I felt that they were closer to me than were the other children because I was the first outsider they had known. They were eager to please, anxious to learn, and proud of their progress.

They came to school scrubbed and smiling, and sat at their desks or around the library table, which was an old kitchen table Ed had lowered by sawing off a few inches from the legs, and for which the older boys had built benches. As they listened to me, their fur-clad feet swung back and forth. Their hair, which I cut twice a month, was combed straight back. Gus and George kept theirs closely cut; Olia, Sassa, and Matrona had bangs; and only Chunook wore his long. As I looked at the neat, crisp braids of one of the girls, I saw something move. Quickly, I glanced from head to head, and each told the same story. I spoke quickly but calmly.

"Anecia, will you come help the first graders for a minute, please?"

While she worked with the children, I stepped to the medicine cabinet to retrieve the green medical book, then went to the living room, where Ed was working on reindeer reports. We consulted the index, turned to the listed page and soon saw what was making the children's skulls crawl. There was an enlarged picture of a head louse.

Ed returned with me to the classroom, and together we made the rounds, up one row and down the next, inspecting heads. There were twelve infected children.

Ed turned to me. "We'll have to wash them after school."

I recalled the words of the green book: "Soak the hair for a few minutes in kerosene, then wash well."

We would have to carry water from the spring, heat it on the kitchen range, then wash the children's hair in granite basins.

"It won't take long," I said. "We'll wash them here in the schoolroom and dry them with paper towels."

Countless times I had cut their hair and never seen anything resembling lice. Anecia explained that since they always knew a day in advance when I would be cutting their hair, they had a chance to wash it. Washing removed the creatures but not the nits, or eggs. Only kerosene would do that.

I remembered that at Kanakanak, when a child came to the orphanage from a village, his hair was quickly clipped short. The youngsters of Kulukak knew this, and wanted to avoid such hurt and humiliation. We wanted to keep their love and confidence, so kerosene was the only solution.

That afternoon Ed poured kerosene on their heads, and I washed it out after a few minutes. Anecia stood beside the big stove and dried them with paper towels. Ed winked at me when little George was embarrassed about the *schoolarista* washing his hair.

But infestation with lice was not the only affliction that ran rampant among the children. I soon discovered scabies, a contagious skin disease accompanied by intense itching. More than once Ed carried water from the spring, heated it in the washboiler on the range, carried it to the classroom, and poured it into our galvanized "itch tub." Behind the stove the afflicted youngster would disrobe and soak with a bar of yellow laundry soap. To loosen the scabs, there followed a rubbing with the "itch brush," which once had been my vegetable brush but which Ed insisted was more urgently needed for the children's hygiene. Then, standing in the tub like Botticelli's *Birth of Venus*, the child was dried off with paper towels, and I covered the infected spots with sulphur ointment.

The youngsters hated to be found with scabies, but when I told them it was catching and explained about the "itch-mite" that burrowed under their skin and laid eggs, they tolerated the cleaning treatment and the disinfectant on their clothes.

Later, when a little girl wasn't in her seat one morning, I made another disturbing discovery.

"Where's Petusa today?" I asked the class.

"She sick," came a response from Michael.

"Where? How sick?"

"Awful sick in the stomach." he said. "Too much chew tobacco."

"Too much what? Michael, are you sure?"

He repeated himself, but I refused to believe him. He went on to say that Petusa chewed often, and even her father, Evon, said she chewed too much. I wondered what he considered the right amount of tobacco for his eight-year-old daughter.

"How long has Petusa chewed?" I asked Michael.

"Maybe one winter and one summer."

I knew the men in the village chewed tobacco, and I had seen old Koopik sitting in the doorway of his *barabara* mixing willow ashes with tobacco to made snuff, but I still refused to believe the children had picked up the habit. I asked Anecia if she had seen Petusa chew.

"Yes," she said. "Petusa sometimes chew. Other boys and girls sometimes chew. Not only Petusa."

"Do you, Anecia?" I asked.

"Long time ago I little bit chew. White teacher tell me not chew. She said very bad. I stop. Some other big girls not stop."

"Anecia, how many children in the room chew tobacco?"

Her eyes scanned the rows of solemn little faces, which were fearful they had displeased their *schoolarista*.

"Maybe eight. I not know how many."

A little questioning revealed that ten youngsters in the class sometimes chewed tobacco. My heart sank. I was at a loss. Kerosene or sulphur ointment wouldn't help here. I decided to drop it for the day, think about it, and organize a way to deal with the problem.

The next day, disregarding college lectures in child psychology, I decided to use the worst kind of motivation—prizes and gifts for rewards. I offered a desired trinket for the girls and pocket knives for the boys if they would stop chewing tobacco. And it worked. The three little boys were fascinated at the thought of possessing knives that opened and closed like Mr. Morgan's, and the girls—especially Petusa—desired strands of colored beads. Then it was only fair that the children who did not chew should receive prizes as well. We made a list of the special longing of each child. All understood that anyone who continued to chew would not receive a reward. Immediately, I sent another plea and the list to my family.

The days and weeks slipped by, and all but one of the youngsters kept their promise. Morning after morning Petusa reported that she "little bit chew" the evening before. She was indifferent to coaxing and shame, and she couldn't be bought. She spoiled the record for the class, and her older brother and sister let her know they were ashamed of her. Finally, for a period of two months, Petusa was able to stop. Each morning she walked into the room and proudly announced, while we waited expectantly, "Me not chew."

Just before the end of the school year in spring, the much-awaited package arrived. We made an occasion of it, serving cookies and hot chocolate topped with melting marshmallows. As I gave Annie her bracelet, Lucy her strand of red beads, Petusa her yellow ones, Sophia her green ones, and each boy his pocket knife, I reminded them that only men chew tobacco.

The girls crowded before the mirror, delightedly trying on one another's beads and bracelets. George sat at his desk, in a world of his own, chanting to himself, "Thank you, thank you, thank you" as he opened and closed his very own knife.

8. Christmas

To my students in Kulukak, December meant Christmas, when we had the biggest celebration of the year. They dreamed of the evening party in the schoolroom, the only Christmas festivity they would have. In the days before the party, the children dug in the snow behind the *barabaras* and uncovered mussel shells. The ones that were not chipped or broken were carefully washed and taken to the carpenter shack, where Ed drilled a hole through each brittle shell. Then they drew strands of colored yarn through the holes and tied them securely with loops. Carefully they painted the shells and left them on the library table to be admired until the day when they would adorn the Christmas tree.

The children learned songs and lines for their parts in the school Christmas program. Jimmy and Ilutsik practiced "Silent Night" and "Jingle Bells" on their harmonicas. Anecia struggled with "America the Beautiful" on the old organ, and even the first graders, with their limited English, had parts to play. Little George worked delightedly with his twelve lines, always forgetting at least one despite my prompting and correction.

Jimmy and Ilutsik had seen a single struggling evergreen tree miles from the village, and they would have to travel an entire day by dogsled to get it. But they didn't mind. We needed a tree, and that was the only one to be found.

Ed and I wanted each child to receive a gift from Santa's bag. Thanks to a suggestion made by a former government teacher when we passed through Seattle, we had bought strands of beads, bracelets, and handkerchiefs for the older girls, dolls for the little girls, and harmonicas and balloons for the boys. Anecia and I sewed many evenings, making rag dolls with yarn hair and button eyes for the tots too young to attend school.

As we sewed, Anecia told me how the Eskimos made rattles for the small children by blowing up the craw of a ptarmigan, seeds inside, and allowing it to dry. She told me of the snow knives with long, flat blades carved from walrus tusks and etched with designs on the handles. The knives were used to illustrate stories in the snow while children listened and watched.

The snow knife was the one toy children were allowed to take outdoors in the winter. A display of other toys might anger the winter spirits, causing a long winter and starvation. The children could take dolls and toys outdoors only after the kittiwake was seen in the harbor. This little gull of the arctic, with its white body, gray wings, and black spot on the top of its head, was a welcome herald of spring.

We had no ribbon or Christmas wrapping paper, so Anecia and I made the packages beautiful with yarn and crepe paper. One evening I was preparing dinner as Anecia wrapped presents.

"Schoolarista, this glue not stick," she said.

When she brought it to me and I examined the tube, I had to explain that things other than glue sometimes come in tubes.

"This is Unguentine, an ointment medicine," I said.

When, at last, the day of the party arrived, Jimmy and Ilutsik had returned with the tree, and I had performed my twice-monthly task of cutting hair. The older girls had permission to bring their best dresses to school to be ironed for the evening, and they brought along shirts and dresses belonging to their brothers and sisters as well.

Little Gus had no best shirt, only one that was so patched it was hard to tell which material was original. Worn-out sleeves had been replaced with extensions of tan cloth, and the tan was spotted with patches of plaid gingham. His family was one of the poorest in the village. Petusa, his younger sister, had only one patched, ragged dress. For perhaps the fifth time, I explored my dwindling wardrobe, found an apron I could spare, and combined it with muslin to make into a jumper for Petusa. Then I remembered a pair of Ed's pajamas that could be transformed into a shirt for Gus, and the older girls and I went to work. When Gus marched into the carpenter shack to show Ed his new shirt, and Petusa stood happily smoothing her dress, their delight couldn't possibly have equaled mine.

That afternoon the older girls popped corn, and Ed and I made seventy-five popcorn balls and filled seventy-five paper bags with nuts, raisins, and candy for each person, adult or child, who came to the party.

The schoolroom was warm, with the homely, bulbous heater making up in efficiency what it lacked in appearance. Two Coleman lanterns hung from the ceiling. A red bell swung in the center of the room, and paper Santa Clauses stood around the top of the blackboard. The Christmas tree, laden with popcorn strings, painted mussel shells, and several time-worn ornaments, stood in the corner.

Ed rang the bell at seven, and instantly people swarmed onto the porch. They had been waiting behind the snow drift just beyond the building. Fathers, mothers, children, and babies, all dressed in fur parkas and bringing with them the now-familar odor of fish, grass smoke, and seal oil, settled in the school seats.

Peter's wife, Maluk, came over to me with Baby Matrona. The child, looking like a doll in her squirrelskin parka, smiled and held out her hand. It bled from a small scratch. When I picked her up and she put her arms around my neck, I thought she was the loveliest Eskimo child I had seen.

Peter walked over.

"Baby Matrona needs a little bandage," he said.

Ed took them to the living quarters.

The youngsters removed their parkas and hung them in the hall. The girls giggled, smoothed their skirts, and whispered. The boys tucked in their shirts and thrust nervous hands into their pockets. Little George couldn't stand still for a minute. I reminded him of his lines, and he smiled, showing a row of white teeth with the front one missing.

"This time I not forget," he promised.

When the program began, twenty-one children stood at the front of the room and sang "America the Beautiful" and "Silent Night" while I pumped the old organ. The audience sat quietly, and the children performed the parts they had practiced so diligently. When finally George stood alone at the front of the room, all was quiet, and his little voice held the attention of the audience. Suddenly his voice stopped, and his hand clapped over his mouth.

"Schoolarista," he stared at me. "I forgetted that line."

At last Santa Claus arrived and removed a bulky bag from his back. The happy smiles and delighted squeals were the only Christmas presents Ed and I needed. We passed out the bags of sweets and chatted with each person as he or she said, "*Quyana*, Schoolarista. *Assirtuq* [good]."

Maluk and Baby Matrona

After the last happy guest left the building, Ed and I took down the lamps and returned to the living quarters. We didn't mind that we were far from our families at Christmas and that we were alone on a hill near the coast of the Bering Sea. Ed laughed when I told him we had forgotten to give out the lollipops wrapped in colored cellophane bought especially for the Christmas party. I fell asleep that Christmas Eve planning a New Year's party where little Eskimo children would lick Christmas lollipops.

9. Child of the Tundra

Because of a child, the shadow of sorrow hung over our village soon after Christmas.

Only the day before, Baby Matrona had stood inside our storm door, clinging to Maluk's hand. In her squirrelskin parka, sealskin boots, and red bandana knotted under her chin, she was a tiny picture of her mother. But Matrona's skin was as light as mine, and wisps of brown hair curled around her forehead. Her eyes, the heritage of a Norwegian fisherman, were unlike those of the other children of the village.

"Baby Matrona sick. Hurt in her heart," explained Anecia, interpreting for Maluk.

We had learned that if an Eskimo suffered a pain anywhere from his neck to his knees, he blamed his heart.

Matrona placed her dirty hands on her abdomen and looked imploringly at Ed when he knelt before her and asked where she hurt. He slipped a thermometer under her tongue while Anecia repeated his instructions to hold it with her lips closed firmly. When someone came for medical aid that was beyond simple remedies or was not in the green book, we did nothing other than offer a glass of fruit juice or milk, a bowl of steaming reindeer broth, or perhaps a loaf of *kelipaq* (warm bread). This was our way of showing understanding and trying to compensate for being teachers when a physician was needed. Sometimes Ed urged someone to make the two-day trip to the doctor in Kanakanak, and the person might go or might not. This, along with placing our trust in the Eskimo gods and our own, was all we could do.

The thermometer registered 102 degrees.

Baby Matrona sipped tomato juice, and Ed announced, "A doctor should see her."

But with the warm weather of the previous few days, the rivers were too dangerous to cross, and dogsled travel was impossible.

"Anecia," Ed said, "tell Maluk to have Baby Matrona drink lots of water and fruit juice and to take another aspirin later today. She should be kept inside and quiet."

Hugging the can of juice, Matrona shuffled out of the building and down the hill with her mother. She seemed hardly big enough to be four years old. I wondered what life held for her.

Later in the day, when Ed was in the village, he called to Peter, asking about the baby. Peter stopped his work on a broken sled. "She seems all right now," he said. "She drank the juice and had some soup." Then he added, "She just ate too much."

In the small hours that night we were awakened by frantic pounding on the storm door. Ed opened it to find the boy Ilutsik.

"Peter say come. Baby Matrona."

While we dressed, he came to us again, urging, "*Qemitaanritek* [make haste, you two]!"

Pulling on parkas, caps, and fur boots, we took flashlights and hurried down the hill to Peter and Maluk's *barabara*. We crouched to enter the outer doorway and take several steps through the dark tunnel before entering a room of heavy, humid, smothering odors of raw hides, grass smoke, boiling fish, and people.

Baby Matrona lay on one of the straw-covered bunks that lined both sides of the room. Old Mollia, her wrinkled, brown grandmother, sat cross-legged at her feet. Peter leaned over his child, his shirt soaked between his shoulders. The child did not look like Matrona. She was still wearing her parka and fur boots, but her face and body were swollen, and she had dark blue blotches on her face. She was comatose and breathing hard. Her family turned to us in hopes that we could help the baby. Somehow I knew Baby Matrona would die.

The stuffiness, the late hour, our helplessness, and the closeness of death made the room swim before me. I turned and made my way back outside, where I prayed for a way to help Baby Matrona and to comfort Peter and Maluk. I couldn't remain away, however, and slowly returned to the hut.

The anxious eyes of father, mother, and grandmother turned as I entered. The baby's loud, labored breathing went on, and Peter gave Ed and me a questioning, troubled look.

Ed shook his head. "We don't know, Peter."

Hesitantly and questioningly, Peter whispered, "Very bad, Schoolarista?"

"Yes, Peter. Very bad."

Peter ran his fingers through his hair and turned back to his child, pushing the damp curls from her forehead. It seemed as if he were trying to give her some of his own strength. Old Mollia's eyes were on Matrona. She shook her head and muttered softly to herself in Yup'ik. People silently slipped into the room, watched the stricken child, then slipped out again.

Suddenly Peter signaled Ed to come close. The child stirred, and Maluk rose to her feet. Baby Matrona opened unseeing eyes, turned her body, threw her arms

out, and struggled to rise. Quickly, Peter slipped his
arm under her shoulders, and she pulled herself up.

Then her body sagged limply, and she collapsed. Gently, Peter placed her back on the bed of dry grass and
bent over her. He dropped to the bunk with his head
in his hands. Maluk sobbed silently, and Old Mollia,
wringing her hands, moaned. I moved to the bunk near
Peter, not knowing how, through the barrier of a language I did not know, to comfort a parent who has lost
a child.

Soon Peter's sobbing stopped, and he turned to Ed.

"Maybe, Schoolarista, you have boards to make box?"

"In the carpenter shack. Whatever you want. I'll help
you."

Inadequately, I expressed my thoughts. "Peter, tell
Maluk we're deeply sorry. Tell her I have a soft, warm
blanket to line the box."

Speaking quietly in Yup'ik, he gave her my message.
Maluk turned to me, nodded her head, and whispered,
"*Quyana*, Schoolarista."

The next day Peter gently lifted Baby Matrona into
the little coffin he and Ed had built. It was just forty
inches long, made of rough lumber. There on the sod
floor of the *barabara* the coffin rested while the men
dug a grave in the frozen ground outside. The snow
swept down, all but obliterating the figures as they
dug from the surface, prevented by superstition from
stepping down into the grave.

The men lowered the plain little box into the grave,
and Peter gently tossed Matrona's meager clothing, fur
boots, and toys on top. Maluk, Peter, and Old Mollia, in
reindeerskin parkas, stood huddled together. Each in
turn scattered a handful of sod on the coffin before the
men covered it over. Maluk, her pale face framed in a
black bandana, stood with her hands tightly clasped.

That afternoon, I looked at the endless tundra and

gray skies, and I thought of the child's needless death and of our helplessness. A few days before, I had read an author who said that the existence of a just and all-seeing God is proved by the beauty of nature's hills, flowers, and trees. In my bitterness, I could almost see the man who wrote those words as he sat in a comfortable home with his children well-fed, within reach of quality medical care, warmly clothed, and never knowing life without its comforts and luxuries. I wondered what he would have written if he had stood helpless in that sod dwelling and had seen the pitiful funeral and the little grave in the frosted earth.

10. Tourist Season

A few days before Christmas a dogsled had come down the trail from Togiak. We watched the sled glide easily over the snow, dogs barking and carrying their tails like plumes as they pulled. The driver ran behind the sled, his mittened hands gripping the handlebars. Peter had recently remarked that the weather was right for travel, the snow deep, and the rivers frozen over.

After a few minutes, George appeared at our door with a note the traveler had carried from the Togiak teachers, Mr. and Mrs. Schrammeck. Their son Wallace was ill with a chronic stomach ailment, and Mr. Schrammeck planned to be along later in the day en route to Kanakanak to talk with the doctor.

We were excited at the idea of seeing another person from the States and for the opportunity to send the stack of letters I had been writing to the family. We could even send a telegram home for Christmas.

I flew for paper and pencil, and we composed a fifty-word night letter. Quickly, I got things together for a hot meal for our visitor, whenever he would arrive. Then I sat at my typewriter and composed another letter to the family. But our anxious waiting was to no avail. Mr. Schrammeck did not arrive that day or the next. We grew uneasy, but Peter assured us Mr. Schrammeck had lived in this country for many years and had traveled the staked trail countless times. Perhaps, too, the child's health was improved. We hoped for the latter as our hopes of sending a Christmas message faded.

A few days later an Eskimo man, unknown to us, came in the front door without knocking, and walked through the hall and living room into the kitchen, where Ed and I were. He set down a large, bumpy gunnysack near the stove, then handed Ed a letter from Mr. Schrammeck. The letter explained that Wallace was very ill, and both parents would arrive with him in a few days. Mrs. Schrammeck was prepared to fly Outside with Wallace if the doctor advised it. I was very eager for their arrival.

Soon after the traveler left, Ed and I noticed a heavy odor of burned fish permeating the house. We took the flashlight and investigated, and our noses led us to the gunnysack by the stove. Ed opened the top, and we had our first look at the dried salmon that travelers use for dog food in Alaska. The fish was dark and dry, and each side was cut with two slashes. Mr. Schrammeck had sent the salmon ahead for his dogs. The hair on Spike's shoulders stood on end, and Ed hurriedly carried the sack to the coal shed.

One evening, after we had given them up for the day, Mr. Schrammeck, his wife, and Wallace arrived on two sleds. One was driven by Mr. Schrammeck, while his wife and son rode in the basket bundled in furs. An Eskimo accompanied them, driving the other sled, which carried luggage and dried fish.

While Ed helped unharness and stake out the dogs, I brought Mrs. Schrammeck and Wallace inside. The child was pale and listless. He toyed with his food as his parents fussed over him. Mr. Schrammeck was quiet, tall, and soft-spoken; Mrs. Schrammeck was friendly and helpful. They were much older than Ed and me, and, Peter told us, they were deeply religious.

We talked for hours that night and the following day about the ways of the Eskimos, of the reindeer work, and of our work as government teachers. I learned, for example—and to my dismay—that urine had been used to tan the skins of my beautiful new fur boots. We talked about the medical aspects of our work, and of how to cope with the *piivaq* barrel.

The weather was clear and cold the morning our guests left for Kanakanak with our mail and telegram to the family. Mr. Schrammeck drove a team of seven gray malamutes. The two teams moved across the tundra and disappeared with amazing swiftness. Ed's thoughts were on the dogs and sled.

"In this country," he said, "a man needs a dogteam."

As the days passed, we watched the frozen bay for return of the teams that would bring our first mail from home. When they did arrive, with Wallace seemingly improved, our joy at receiving more than a hundred letters (none from Cousin Edgar) was eclipsed by the sad news that just a week before, Mace had been killed.

An Alaska Airways plane taking off from Kanakanak for Anchorage had broken a strut in the bumpy snow. The pilot, with help from some of the people there, built a tripod of iron pipes tied at the top with one-inch manila rope to lift the plane. The tripod collapsed, and one of the pipes struck Mace on the head, knocking him unconscious. When he came to, he was able to walk the five hundred feet to the hospital, and for a short time appeared normal, suffering only a slight headache. Then he lost consciousness again and died at midnight. His body was taken by plane to Anchorage and shipped from there to the home of his parents in Iowa. He was twenty-eight years old.

Ed stared out the window. "I wonder if Mace would

have wanted his body shipped Outside," he said. "I wouldn't have."

All the letters except for the last one from Grandmother, which Ed and I eagerly read during a few stolen moments, lay on the desk unopened during the day the Schrammeck family remained with us. After the teams disappeared over the hill, Ed and I quickly made a pot of coffee and settled ourselves in the living room to enjoy the delightful luxury of our letters. After arranging them in chronological order, I read while Ed listened, then Ed read while I listened. It took until dinnertime to read the entire stack.

There was one interruption. Stephan, the little third grader, came to the door distressed. He stepped into the hall, pulled up his parka, turned his back to us, and pulled down his jeans to expose a red gash, blood-caked and dried, across his bottom.

"Stephan," I cried, "how did that happen?"

"Falled on reindeer horn. Hurts much."

Ed cleaned and dressed the wound, and Stephan left, munching a candy bar.

Later that evening, Ed and I stood outside our back door, enjoying the full moon and the starlit night.

"Homesick?" he asked.

"No, not really. I'd rather be here than any place I know."

"And so would I."

"But I find comfort in the thought that the same moon shines in Grandmother's bedroom window tonight, and the same sky is a roof over us all."

Our next visitor arrived unannounced. Ed and Spike had just returned from a day of ptarmigan hunting, and the dog lay exhausted behind the stove. Suddenly we heard confusion and yelping. Ed pulled on his jacket and went outside. A moment later he dashed in for the lantern.

"We've got a visitor," he said. "I'll help him stake out

his dogs. We'll have to get fish for them from the village. It'll take twenty minutes or so. Can you hold dinner?"

I had just added coal to the firebox to heat water for dishes. I pulled the kettles and skillet to the back of the range, put grids under them, and opened the oven door. Anecia set another place at the table.

Ed entered the kitchen with a red-faced, middle-aged man.

"Abbie, this is Mr. Johnson. He's traveling through here on his way to Goodnews Bay."

Our visitor shook my hand, then went to the stove to warm himself. He wore a squirrelskin parka, fur cap, and hair-seal boots from which snow melted on my clean floor. While Mr. Johnson washed for dinner, Ed nodded toward the skillet of ptarmigan and whispered, "Hope he isn't the game warden."

I recalled that a hunting license cost fifty dollars for a nonresident and a person was classed as such until he had lived in the territory for a year. I thought of the fines for poaching game and of Ed's serving time sitting it out at the marshal's. The man reappeared in the kitchen with face clean and hair neatly combed.

"Been getting many ptarmigan?" he asked.

"Quite a few lately," Ed said. "Probably the reason the Eskimos haven't brought in any reindeer."

"Get these yourself?"

"Yes. I got two today."

We sat down at the table, with a platter of ptarmigan as mountainous as a turkey.

"What kind of gun are you using?"

"I used a twelve-gauge shotgun."

"Been doing any other hunting?"

I couldn't stand it any longer. Turning to him, I demanded, "Are you the game warden?"

The man was startled. "Me, the game warden? Hell, no, lady. I'm just an ol' sourdough mushing my way to the coast."

He threw back his head, laughed heartily, and helped himself to more ptarmigan.

Peter came up one morning to ask Ed to make the trip to Dillingham with him the next day. The following evening, while Ed was gone, Paddy Owen, a trader who lived between Kulukak and Togiak, came through en route to Nushagak with a load of furs. He spoke English and came to the station to ask if I would like to see his furs. Chris had told him we wanted to buy mink pelts for gifts to send to our family. He placed fox (red, white, and cross), mink, and ermine pelts across our living room floor and chairs. A sharp, strong odor filled the room. With Anecia and Paddy's help, I chose six mink—two each for my sister, my mother, and Ed's favorite aunt.

As Paddy left, he remarked, "I'll see Mr. Morgan and Peter over on the Nushagak. We'll probably come back together."

The first night Anecia and I were alone was an eventful one. Choking and smothering, I awoke in the night to find the house filled with smoke. Quickly, I awoke Anecia, and we discovered that I had closed the damper of the stove too tightly. Anecia stood at one open door while I stood at the other, waiting for the smoke to clear.

We had just settled back into our beds when we were startled by Spike's snarls and growls. I slipped out of bed and found him with his front feet on the bedroom windowsill and his nose at the open crack.

"What do you think it is, Anecia? A loose dog?"

"Maybe people drinking," she said. "Maybe come up here. Maybe could be *carayak*."

"Anecia, none of that. Not when we're alone."

We listened. Then we heard it. The front storm door had broken loose and was banging in the wind. While Anecia stood in the doorway holding the flashlight with one hand and Spike with the other, I stepped out into the swirling snow and secured the door.

Anecia was not accustomed to night latches. One morning she had followed me into the schoolroom when I went to build a fire, and she closed the hall door behind her, locking us out of the living quarters. In our pajamas, at eighteen degrees below zero in knee-deep snow, we rushed around the house and through the back door.

After five days, we warmly welcomed Ed back home. The weather had turned warm, the trails were slush, and he was wet and cold.

Ed and Peter had arrived at the hospital amidst talk of organizing a search party for them. Paddy had gone straight there, while Ed and Peter had gone first to Snag Point. When Paddy appeared and announced that Ed and Peter had departed from Kulukak the day before, the people at Kanakanak were alarmed.

"You know," he said to me his first night back, "the light from our living room window shines clear across the bay. It's a wonderful beacon, and it's a welcome sight. You're nearly home when you see it."

And Ed had, at last, heard word of Cousin Edgar. With two companions, Edgar was at Tikchik Lakes trapping marten and beaver. About the time we had arrived at Kanakanak the previous fall, he and his friends had left for the lakes, where they would remain until spring. A plane was taking provisions to them sometime during the winter, so Ed had left a letter to go along.

The Schrammeck family had been gone less than a week when, one evening, Mr. Schrammeck returned to Kulukak on his way to Kanakanak to get more medicine for Wallace. The weather had turned warm, and rain was pouring down. Mr. Schrammeck spent the night in the schoolroom, where he kept a fire to dry his clothes. The next morning glare ice covered the tundra but, eager to be on the trail, the nine dogs of his team barked impatiently as he harnessed them.

Four days later an Eskimo hurriedly arrived from Togiak with instructions from Mrs. Schrammeck that he meet her husband on his return with the medicine and have him turn back for the doctor. Wallace was desperately ill. Shortly after the messenger arrived, Mr. Schrammeck pulled up to the station. He was weary and worried, and his dogs were too tired to leave again so soon.

Peter came in. "I'll go," he said. "My dogs are fresh, and I'll travel light and make good time. I'll be there in the morning."

The weather had turned cold again, with the thermometer hovering around twenty below zero, and the wind was strong. Mr. Schrammeck wearily ate a hot lunch while his socks and mittens dried by the range. He, too, planned to drive all night, back to Togiak.

As he started to leave, I noticed a heavy sock on one of the chairs.

"Is that yours?"

Resignedly, he nodded, came back in, patiently untied and removed his pack boot, and put on the sock. I marvelled at his forbearance and regretted he wasn't a swearing man. It would have helped then.

Early the next afternoon, two teams came across the bay. Through the binoculars, we recognized one as Peter's, and as the other drew up alongside the station, I counted in it thirteen malamutes, their sides heaving, their tongues lolling, their breath making white clouds as they dropped in the snow. The driver helped the doctor from the sled,

While traveling in the moonlight the previous night, Peter had noticed a light at a cabin a mile off the staked trail. There, he found the doctor already headed our way, toward Togiak. The doctor was such a big, jovial

man that I found myself forgiving him for flicking ciga-
rette ashes on the floor and crushing the butt with his
heel.

After the dogs were staked and the men had a hot
meal, Anecia and I made the rounds among the *barabaras*, bidding all the people who were ailing, and all
mothers with young children, to come to the station to
see the doctor.

The *tyone* of the Eskimos in our area was the first to
pound on the door. He had earlier that day sent Michael
to Ed for medicine for a boil on his abdomen. The *tyone*
was a handsome man, extremely reserved. He walked
hesitantly into the living room, holding up his squirrelskin parka. The doctor took him into the schoolroom
to examine the boil, and when he was finished, the
tyone's stomach was bulging with dressings. As he left,
the doctor teasingly called, "Maybe pretty soon you'll
have a baby." The *tyone*, like all the Eskimos, was as
quick to laugh at a joke on himself as on anyone else.

Carefully, the doctor examined each person who had
come for treatment and carefully checked each baby
and small child in the village. Anxious to leave the next
morning for Togiak to tend to Wallace, he promised to
examine the school youngsters on his return trip.

The doctor also took time to talk to Anecia about her
problem with Alexie and Koopcha.

"Koopcha drinks," he told Anecia. "And when he's
drinking, he's mean. Don't marry him."

Then he finished with an offer of work for Anecia in
Kanakanak.

"We need a nurse's aide at the hospital, a girl who
can speak English. How would you like to come over
there and work with us?"

As was her way, Anecia considered the offer quietly
for several minutes, then said, "I like it, but I like it
here, too, to live with the *schoolaristas*."

We explained to her that in the coming summer I

planned to go Outside, and it was possible that we would no longer be in Kulukak the following winter. Teachers were transferred frequently. All of us agreed that Anecia should be away from the village, so we decided that in the spring, when I left to visit in the States, Anecia would go along to Kanakanak and remain working at the hospital.

The doctor was at Togiak for more than a week. He told us that on the night Mr. Schrammeck left Kulukak for his village, his dogs had chased a fox and, in the darkness, Mr. Schrammeck lost his way. He found himself far out on the ice shelf of Bristol Bay and did not reach home until long after daylight. He lay ill for several days from exposure and fatigue. The doctor remained until he recovered and Wallace's condition improved.

Upon his return to Kulukak, the doctor remained a day with us, thoroughly checking the school children. After examining the last one, he told us, "This is one of the cleanest, healthiest groups I've examined in any village in Alaska."

Four days after the doctor left, an Eskimo from Togiak brought us mail from Nushagak as he went for the doctor again. This time Wallace was so ill the doctor had to send a plane to take him and Mrs. Schrammeck from Togiak to Anchorage, where they could board a ship to seek medical help Outside.

We never knew when a traveler might arrive, stake out his dogs beside the station, sit at our table, and stretch out his sleeping bag in the schoolroom. But we didn't mind. We welcomed the companionship of travelers, and they always brought or took our mail.

11. Daughter of Old Mollia

One cold night in February, Ed and I sat warming our feet on the fluted skirt of the heater, as we listened to the Richfield Reporter, broadcasting from the States. Anecia sat at the desk, writing a letter to a friend. Suddenly there was a knock at the back storm door. Ed let in Jimmie, one of the older boys who had been out on the tundra herding reindeer. He addressed Anecia in Yup'ik.

"Maluk wants medicine," Anecia told Ed.

"What kind of medicine?"

"Aspirin and maybe some ammonia. Maluk fell on the ice. She not feel right. She want to smell that medicine."

Maluk had learned of the use of ammonia when Peter worked as a driver for a government doctor's dogteam.

"Is Maluk hurt badly?" Ed asked.

"Bad hurt here," Anecia said, pointing to her abdomen. "Now not have baby."

Anecia, Jimmie, Ed, and I walked down the hill over the glassy, crusted snow. We entered the *barabara* where Maluk's aged mother lived, and found the room hot and steamy, with the heavy odor of boiling meat and grass smoke. The room was large, with the usual domed ceiling. A small table at the opposite end was littered with dishes and kettles. A stove made from a fifty-gallon gasoline drum belched occasional puffs of smoke. The sod floor was cluttered with fur boots, a quarter of a reindeer, and willow branches for firewood. On one of the low bunks that lined both sides of the room were several children, one asleep, and the others sitting up watching us. On the end of the other bunk Old Mollia, a leathery-skinned little woman, sat cross-legged, sewing a fur boot. Anecia had told me that Old Mollia's husband, now dead, had been a medicine man.

Maluk, in her squirrelskin parka and black scarf, lay on her side near Mollia. Her face rested on one hand, while her feet, in fur boots, were tucked under her parka. Her brown eyes, large and beautiful, showed the pain she suffered. Still, she smiled and answered my greeting with "*Cama-i.*"

Maluk could speak no English, so Anecia interpreted. It seemed that Maluk, several months pregnant, had lost her baby but felt she would be all right in a little while. This had happened to her before. We gave her the aspirin and ammonia and suggested that she lie quietly for several days. The old grandmother broke into the conversation twice, muttering crossly.

"Anecia, what is Old Mollia saying?" I asked.

"She say, 'White man's medicine not good.' She all the time say that. Maybe because Old Mollia's husband was medicine man. He tell Old Mollia white man's medicine not good for Eskimos."

It was pleasant to step into the clear air, to see stars overhead in a clear sky, and to feel the wind blow cold and fresh from the Bering Sea. Laden with bread, reindeer broth, and a hot-water bottle, Anecia and I returned to Old Mollia's *barabara.* Again I urged Maluk not to get up and gather wood or to carry her youngest child on her back.

After Anecia explained how to refill the hot-water

bottle, and Maluk had sipped the broth, Anecia and I left.

"Old Mollia not want Maluk take aspirin," Anecia told me. "She say for us to use old ways and go to medicine man."

Anecia took my hand and led me through the dark tunnel. I later learned that in this entry Old Mollia's husband had seen a dwarf who was believed to have come to cast evil on him. He was seen as the emissary of a shaman with whom Old Mollia's husband had quarreled.

The next day Anecia and I took soup and canned fruit to Maluk. She greeted us cheerfully and said she felt better, but still she wore her parka, fur boots, and head scarf indoors. We were glad when we saw Peter's team come over the hill that afternoon. Later, when he came up to the station, we asked him about Maluk.

"She'll be all right," he said, adding that she always made an unnecessary fuss when she was sick.

The next day, when I suggested to Anecia that we take something down to Maluk, she said, "Maybe you not go."

"Why not?"

"Peter not like white teachers come to Old Mollia's *barabara*. Old Mollia believe in old ways. Sometimes *barabara* and childrens not clean. Maybe Peter a little bit ashame."

Peter was proud. Always when he came to the station he was freshly shaven, his hair combed, and his clothes clean. Anecia had told me one morning, when George was late to school, that Peter had scolded him and sent him home to wash and comb his hair.

In deference to Peter's wishes, I didn't visit Mollia's dwelling, but sent Anecia down to the village with soup and other food that I thought would please Maluk. Whenever Peter was at the station, I inquired about his wife. He always answered that she would be all right. One time he added, "She's lazy."

Two weeks slipped by, and still Maluk kept to her bed. Anecia reported that she looked ill, and that she complained.

"Could she be lazy?" I asked.

Anecia nodded. "All womens know Maluk lazy, but now Maluk sick."

Then, the last of February, three weeks after Maluk's fall, the doctor made his annual visit to the village. Ed told Peter the doctor would come down to see his wife.

Peter shook his head.

"She'll never see the doctor. She'll be all right. This happened before, and she got over it."

Several weeks later, with Maluk still in bed, I decided I had to go see her. I was horrified at what I found. She lay in the same clothes she had on the first night I had seen her after her fall. But she was a different woman. Her fresh, healthy beauty was gone, replaced by sunken cheeks and a ghastly color. Heavy, dark circles made her eyes look too large for her face. Through Anecia, she told me she was very ill.

The room was stifling hot. I loosened my coat and slipped a thermometer between Maluk's parched lips. Old Mollia immediately started muttering. The thermometer registered 102 degrees. Alarmed, I ran to the carpenter shack, where Ed was helping Peter steam the runners of his sled.

"Ed," I said, "Maluk is terribly ill. Peter, something must be done for her right away."

But Peter was unmoved.

"She got over this before," he said. "But she won't listen to anyone but that old woman. I wanted her to let the doctor see her."

"Peter, you've got such a good dogteam. Couldn't you bundle her up well, leave early in the morning, and get her to the hospital by tomorrow night?"

"Sure, I'll take her if she'll go. But she won't go against the old woman." He continued working with the drill, boring holes for screws in the hardwood runners.

That evening, downcast, Peter came to the station and asked if I would go down and try to persuade Maluk to go to the hospital. I found Maluk uneasy, and she emphatically refused to see a doctor.

"*Qang'a*" she said, and closed her eyes to dismiss us.

Beside Maluk on the bunk lay the forefoot of a reindeer, the meat red above the white hair and shiny black hoof.

"Why is that here?" I asked Old Mollia through Anecia.

"Sometimes rub sores with reindeer hoof," she answered. "Sometimes with seal flipper. Sometimes helps to call spirits."

Something had to be done for Maluk. I told Anecia to tell Old Mollia that Maluk would surely die if she didn't go to the hospital. The domineering old woman, through Anecia, answered that the medicine man would cure her daughter.

Peter said it was useless for him to go for the doctor, that Maluk would not talk with him, and that she would not take any medicine prescribed for her. At the insistence of Old Mollia, he sent to another village for a medicine man.

Anecia and I were doing dishes a few days later when she said, "Schoolarista, medicine man in village now. He have Maluk go to *qasgiq*, but she too sick to go. She stay in Old Mollia's *barabara*."

Anecia told me that the medicine man, wearing a strip of walrus gut around his head and covering his face, had knelt on Maluk's bunk. Singing and chanting, he followed the rhythm with his hands and swaying body. When the ritual was over, the family gathered around for food, and the medicine man received fur pelts and dried fish.

"Medicine mans are just like teachers," Anecia told me. "They know about everything—stories, *carayaks*, and things in the ground. But medicine man learns about things in dreams."

Peter was torn between his wife's mother and us, between Eskimo beliefs and modern medicine. He was a part of each culture, yet did not belong completely to either.

Maluk lingered as breakup came and travel became impossible. Ice drifted out of the rivers and creeks, and floating ice prevented travel by boat. Sometimes when Peter was away seal hunting, Maluk sent a youngster to ask for soup, bread, cookies, or canned fruit. Her illness hung like a shadow. Nearly every day either Ed or I took food to her. She complained that her back was covered with sores, but not once in those weeks of illness would she remove her parka. Her cheeks were deeply sunken, her lips were dry, cracked and colorless, and her eyes were in dark hollows. She was ever in my thoughts, and I lay wakeful at night, worried and heartsick. Ed insisted that I not go to see her anymore, so each day Anecia took food to her. Sometimes she ate it, and sometimes she left it untouched.

Peter finally became deeply concerned. He was anxious for us to see her and to do what we could to help. We decided that at first he had not understood how seriously ill she was and had been annoyed with what he took to be habitual laziness and complaining. When he finally did realize how desperately ill she was, her mother dominated the situation.

One morning, the last of April, Spike awakened us early at sounds coming from just over the crest of the knoll, on the tundra. There we could see the heads and shoulders of two men. One was Peter. So this was the end. We knew they were digging a grave. Maluk, who was a beautiful woman in her late twenties and the mother of eight children, would never again carry a child on her back or sit beside a hole in the ice and fish for smelt.

Peter came to the station and sat on a kitchen chair. Ed gave him a cup of coffee.

"Maluk died in the night," he said. "Evon helped me dig a grave. Maybe I could have boards for a box?"

Ed went with him to the carpenter shack, and together they made Maluk's coffin. When it was completed, Peter took it by dogsled to Old Mollia's *barabara*.

Baby Matrona's grave on the tundra didn't appear so lonely now. Her mother had come to lie beside her.

12. The Story of Little Evon, as Told by Anecia

Little Evon stood hesitantly before his parents' gray, mildewed tent. He wore a squirrelskin parka with wolverine ruff, and the long guard hairs around the hood swayed in the raw north wind. His face was stained with tears, and his little square jaw trembled. A small black dog used to herd reindeer stood nearby, watching the boy.

The child glanced fearfully at the silent tundra with its patches of brown earth showing through the melting snow. He stared out to the seal reefs on the horizon and the icy waters of the Bering Sea. This year, to escape their plague-infested village, Evon's parents had come earlier than ever before to the seal grounds and the summer fish camp. He was now alone, though, and had to find his way back to the village.

Softly, he spoke to his dog." *Taitai*, [come], Qimugteq."

The dog trotted beside him, away from the tent, following the tracks left by the runners of his uncle's sled. Evon sobbed. He thought of his parents and, with terror, of the *carayaks*, about whom he had heard his friend Stephan and the old woman Mollia talk. He thought of the village, where people were hushed and frightened because of the recent deaths, and of how he was alone in an endless, silent, white world. He broke into a run with Qimugteq at his heels.

His thoughts swept back over the past few days, when his father had lain ill, and of the morning he had awakened to find his mother leaning over the quiet figure of his father. He had crawled from under the reindeer skins and slipped over beside her. Fearfully, he had turned to his mother and whispered, "My father, he crossed over the River of Tears?"

"*Aang*," his mother nodded.

What were they to do? Could they find the trail back to the village? The ice was going out of the creeks. Could they still cross them? They had no dogteam, no sled, no boat. Wassilia, Evon's uncle, was to come for them in his boat when it was time to leave the summer camp. But they could not remain there after a death and with no one to hunt for food. Evon began to tremble, and he closed his mouth tightly to keep his teeth from chattering.

The top of the tent was sagging because Evon's father had been too ill to drive the stakes into the frozen ground. The gasoline smell from the little stove filled his nose, and he knew that Qimugteq was nearby, for he smelled the dampness of the dog's coat. But above all was the smell of spring, of melting snow and sodden earth. A ptarmigan flew near the tent. Perhaps his mother would make some snares today. She must be very hungry. Then he remembered—his people did not hunt for five days after a death. And he knew his mother was very strict about such things.

Evon wondered what it meant to die. Stephan had told him that it means your spirit leaves your body and never comes back. You no longer matter, only your spirit does. It crosses the River of Tears and never crosses back again. Then it meets the spirits of all the animals you have ever seen during your life. If you have

been good to them, they will be kind to you and help
you in your travels. But if you have been unkind, they
will torment you. The medicine man said to put a morsel
of fish in the dead fox's mouth before you skin it, and to
leave the claws on the carcass so the spirit will be
satisfied. And that is why hunters pour a little fresh
water into the throat of the seal before they skin it. All
this Stephan had said.

Evon's father had been a great hunter. He would see
many animals as he crossed the River of Tears. And,
the medicine man had said, there is a special heaven
for people who have starved to death.

Suddenly his mother was speaking to him.

"Help me, Evon. We'll cover your father with reindeer
skins. Give me one of yours."

"Now will we go back to the village?" Evon asked
hopefully.

"Maybe soon. But I want to sleep now."

She dropped down on Evon's hides as though she were
very weary and, scarcely covering herself, unmindful
of the child beside her, she dropped off to sleep.

Evon watched his mother, then sat on a hide near her
head, waiting for her to waken. He looked at the figure
of his father under the hides and remembered what Old
Mollia and Stephan had hold him about *carayaks*. And
now, if he and his mother stayed in this tent, the *carayaks* would be displeased and maybe he and his mother
would die, too.

Evon's mother was breathing loudly and her face had
an unusual color. She had not eaten for days. Would
she die, too? No, she had to be all right. Soon they would
start back to the village.

"Little Evon," she said weakly, "maybe I, too, will
cross the River of Tears. You will be alone. It is far to
the village. Maybe two days and one night you will
walk. If I sleep long and quiet, like your father, you

must go to your uncle. Take Qimugteq. Follow the sled tracks, and you will find your way from one marker to the next. Do not stop or sleep. If you do, you, too, may cross the River of Tears. Ice is rotten over creeks. You must be careful."

Evon was terrified. "I'll stay here. I won't go."

Her last words to him had been: "Yes, till I sleep quiet. Then you go. You are a brave boy, Evon. Brave like your father."

Now, as Evon traveled, the half light of the Alaska spring evening was closing over the tundra, adding to his feeling of gloom. He walked swiftly between the runner tracks. He knew he must not lose the tracks, or he would be hopelessly lost. But would he be able to see them at night?

"Maybe tonight won't be very dark," he thought. He kept looking back and tried to keep Qimugteq close. In marshes the snow had melted, leaving the ground soggy under the frozen crust. Sometimes he broke through into ankle-deep water.

A ptarmigan darted up in front of him, causing him to scream in fright. Qimugteq dashed after it, barking. As the boy watched it fly, he remembered he was hungry. He stopped for a moment to rest. The dog, panting, dropped on the snow at his feet. The moon was not near that distant hill any longer. It was now high above.

Suddenly Qimugteq stood alert, and Evon watched him. The dog turned his head, growled, then sat on his haunches. Then Evon heard the sound, and in the distance saw a dark blotch with ragged edges moving slowly up a hill. He listened intently, and the wind brought the sound of antlers hitting antlers. The reindeer herd! Suddenly he felt less alone. At least there were some other living creatures in this vast, bleak wilderness.

Concentrating on the sled tracks, he trudged along.

He thought of Wassilia, his mother's brother, who was an ivory carver. He would like to live with Wassilia now that he could not live with his parents.

At the top of a hill he saw what looked like a tripod marker on the staked trail. Forgetting his weariness, he ran in the direction of the tripod, disregarding the sled tracks. Then he hesitated. With terror, he found himself in an old cemetery. What he had seen was not a tripod but a grave marker. He stood motionless. No one ever went near a grave in the dark. *Carayaks* hovered about.

Then, with darkness fading into the steel gray of morning, something moved behind him. It moved nearer, and he fell to the ground screaming.

Then above his sobs, he heard his name and his mother's words: "You are a brave boy, Evon. Brave like your father."

He swallowed hard and got to his feet. His eyes gave a searching glance, as though he expected to see his mother standing there. Suddenly he was no longer afraid. He knew his mother's spirit was with him. Confidently, he retraced his steps, for he knew he must get back to the sled tracks.

All day he walked, Qimugteq beside him. Once, at a creek, he remembered his mother's warning about rotten spring ice, and he left the tracks and trudged a mile upriver to where he could cross on firm ice. Then he followed back in the opposite direction to return to the parallel tracks. Toward evening, when his body ached from weariness and hunger, he saw a team traveling toward him. Too tired to run, he stood still as it approached. Before he could recognize the driver, he heard his name.

"Evon!"

It was Wassilia. Evon sank down in the snow, sobbing.

"Evon, why are you here?"

"My father, my mother, they crossed the River of Tears. My mother said to come to you. For a long time I walked."

"Your father was sick when I brought you to the summer camp," Wassilia said. "All the time I thought about him. I was coming to see if he was all right. The government doctor is in the village. He is helping people. Are you sure, Evon—your mother is dead, too?"

Wassilia placed the child on the basket of the sled and tucked reindeer hides around him.

"We'll go back to the village now," he said. "Another day I'll go to the fish camp. We'll get food for you. Maybe, Evon, you would like to be my boy now? I need a brave boy to help me fish and hunt."

"*Aang*," Evon whispered as he dropped off to sleep. "I be glad."

13. Mush!

Ed had said, "In this country, a man needs a dogteam."

It seemed a simple thing to have, until we realized that metal strips for the runners would have to come on the *North Star* and the sled would have to be built. Dogs were plentiful and prolific, but they had to eat, and in this country they ate dried salmon. The fish had to be caught and cured, and that required a net, a boat, and a smokehouse. Two thousand salmon were needed to feed a team of seven dogs for nine or ten months. Dogs also must have collars and chains, harnesses, and towlines. All that had to come from Outside.

So a simple thing quickly became an involved and complicated undertaking. In preparation for a dogteam to be acquired our second winter in Kulukak, Ed built his boat the preceding spring and learned all he could about sled dogs, for a musher chooses his dogs as carefully as a purchaser chooses the make and color of his automobile. For the proud and particular owner, the dogs must be of the same breed, size, and color. Both Peter's and Mr. Schrammeck's teams were comprised of big gray malamutes. They were magnificent; the dogs'

110

tails waved over their backs like handsome plumes as they ran through Kulukak during our first winter.

The bigger and tougher a dog's feet, the better. Hair between the pads was bad because it tended to gather snow, which turned to ice and then caused cuts and bleeding. Mushers carried gunnysacks in their sleds for such an emergency. Only by putting a dog in the sack, head out, was it possible to keep it from struggling to run with the others. And careful mushers never started on the trail without dog boots, which were canvas stockings that tied securely around the lower leg to protect tender, bleeding feet. A sled dog had to be alert and possess boundless energy as well as unlimited endurance.

Names were chosen as carefully as the dogs. Peter named his after comic strip characters—Min, Andy, Jiggs, Jumbo, Hans, Fritz, and Katie. One musher on the Nushagak named his dogs after movie stars, and another chose the names of liquors. Vodka was his leader.

But we learned that selecting dogs was no job for cheechakos, for those new to mushing took the culls, dogs that no one else wanted to go to the trouble of feeding all summer.

Mr. Schrammeck, when traveling through Kulukak, gave us our first sled dog, a handsome gray malamute named Judy. Two days later, before we had even got acquainted with her, Ed looked up from the breakfast table to see Chris's team going over the crest of the hill, headed for Togiak with Judy tied to the sled. An embarrassed Chris later explained that he had seen Judy and supposed that Mr. Schrammeck had forgotten her, so he took her home, only to have to return her to us. Judy had been trained as a leader, but we eventually replaced her with a younger dog.

Wassilia appeared at the station one day with a gray

pup that he wanted to exchange for flour and milk. Ed made the trade for the thin, mangy little pup named Sandy, and for days the dog scarcely stopped eating.

In April Mr. Schrammack gave us two more dogs—Jumbo, who was ready for retirement, and Tony, who was huge and handsome as well as lazy and loveable—and a white pup we named Rowdy.

Then Peter's dog Katie had pups sired, Peter said, by a handsome gray malamute that belonged to Chris. Three of the pups became ours. They were fat and warm and cuddly, and we played with them by the hour. But they were black, not gray, and they had high dewclaws. No malamute had high dewclaws, and no malamute was black, but Scamp, Jinks, and Sambo made up in mischief and playfulness what they lacked in heritage. They romped around the station and followed us every time we stepped outside.

Peter, with a glance in my direction, told Ed, "Sled dogs don't make house pets. The Schoolarista shouldn't make pets out of them. They won't work if they're overfed."

And Chris, after telling us of the heavens through which a spirit passed after crossing the River of Tears, remarked, "Schoolarista, you'll never get past dog heaven."

We soon learned why no one summered a useless dog. Ed spent hours rustling and preparing dogfood. He cooked smelt, which Shaky Andrew's wife had given to us in exchange for the bread and soup I made for Andrew. He cooked a conglomeration of seal blubber, water, corn meal, and seal oil that was enough to make any dog's mouth water. Peter came in from Herring Bay and brought us two gunnysacks of herring. Ed set up a makeshift stove behind the carpenter shack on which to cook walrus meat an Eskimo had brought in. He built the fire high, and soon the dry grass was ablaze and the wind blew the fire out of control. Ed moved the

Kulukak station with carpenter shack in winter. The stakes in the foreground provide places to chain sled dogs, either ours or those belonging to travelers.

dogs and fought the fire with a wet gunnysack, but the flames spread rapidly. Neither the station nor the village was in danger, but the blaze and smoke were terrifying to see. Anecia and I hurriedly soaked gunnysacks and helped fight the flames. A stranger paddled his kayak across the harbor and told Anecia in Yup'ik to give him a wet gunny sack. After the fire had spread nearly a mile, the wind suddenly changed and we brought the flames under control.

The man who had helped put out the fire stayed to eat dinner with us, and Ed gave him a pound of tea, six cans of condensed milk, two pairs of canvas gloves, and a bag of candy, all of which he smilingly and gratefully accepted. He told Anecia he had known that all the people from the village were at seal camp, so he paddled three miles to help us fight the fire. Because the tide was out when he was ready to leave, he walked the four miles back to his home, planning to return for his kayak the next day at flood tide. His happy, friendly nature was typical of all the Eskimos, and as I watched him leave, I felt love for all of them.

One stormy, windy morning we awoke to find two of the pups gone. Ed spent hours searching and finally found them on a ledge halfway down the cliff near the beach. They had whined pitifully when he walked along the water's edge below the narrow shelf. He climbed up the steep wall and retrieved the wet, hungry pups, and they ate voraciously when they reached home. A few days later, Spike took them down to the beach and returned home without them. After a long hunt in the wind and rain, Ed found them and, with a swat, quickly taught them the meaning of "Go home."

One day, before the salmon were running and Ed was in desperate need of food for the dogs, he told Anecia and me he was going seal hunting the next morning.

"I'm certain I can get a seal with the Winchester 30-30 if I can just get close enough to hit it."

Anecia sent us into gales of laughter by asking softly, "Which end of the gun are you going to hit it with?"

One dog, Tony, took to howling in a low, plaintive, drawn-out wail that mournfully faded away. The cry seemed to tell of the loneliness of this vast country. Sometimes I, too, was lonely, with no books, magazines, or radio, no other women from Outside, and Ed busy with his work. I petted Tony when he howled, and took him a choice morsel of food. But Ed insisted that the mournful wails must cease, and at Mr. Schrammeck's suggestion (and over my protests), he swatted the dog.

"Remember," he said to me, "Spike is yours, and those useless pups. But the sled dogs are mine."

Returning to the kitchen one afternoon, Ed teasingly

put a piece of ice against my neck. I screamed, and instantly all was in confusion. Spike, to our horror, flew at Ed and bit him on the arm, then, with ears down, slunk behind the stove. As I dressed Ed's wound, I was sorry and shocked that Spike had attacked him, but I couldn't help feeling that Ed had deserved a good bite. It evened things up with Tony, who still had my sympathies.

Before the snow melted completely, Ed, for the first time, harnessed Judy, Tony, and Jumbo to an old sled of Peter's to go to the beach and haul up our remaining sacks of coal. As I stood at the door, Peter helped him harness the dogs in the backyard, and Ed stood on the sled and called a loud "Mush." The dogs ran straight for the house, and Judy plunged through the screen door in an attempt to follow me into the kitchen. Before Ed could prevent it, the sled wedged itself in the door frame, with the dogs hopelessly tangled in the traces and towline. Peter, as he helped Ed free the sled, said only, "Long time ago I told you not to let the Schoolarista make pets out of the sled dogs."

Mr. Schrammeck remarked later that if Ed wanted his dogs to travel, he would have to get me to run ahead of the sled.

Ed was furious. After the tangle of dogs, sled, and screen door was finally separated, he came into the kitchen. He had never looked at me like that before, and it was not a look of love. Taking hold of my arm, he said slowly and deliberately, "Will you understand that the sled dogs are mine, and are not to be made into pets?" I knew, of course, that Ed was right.

In early fall, Judy had pups sired by Spike. They were cuddly little mites with squinty eyes, wrinkled noses, and velvet coats. Mr. Schrammeck had warned us that we must dispose of any dogs with short hair because they would never endure the cold of the trail. And neither would any dog with small, hard foot pads, because

Spike and I at Kulukak

Sled and dogs at the Kulukak station

his feet would always be cut and bleeding. We hoped the pups would have Judy's heavy, long coat and big, soft feet, and Spike's alertness and intelligence.

Spike had made friends of everyone in the village, and even Evon now wanted a couple of pups from our litter. But he didn't care for his dogs as we felt he should and we didn't want to give him any of our pups. Where our dogs had long runways, his were fastened to stakes on short chains, and sometimes in the summer his dogs howled pitifully for water and many times had little food. One evening we found one dog, Scamp, lying dead after he had slipped his collar and caught the chain around his neck, strangling himself.

Peter, who also wanted a couple of the pups, took pride in his team and cared for his dogs. Judy's pups were fat and playful, and they ate greedily the food Ed cooked for them, then licked the surplus from one another's faces.

Two long-haired pups we later gave to Peter, a short-haired one we sent to a friend at Kanakanak for a house pet, and three we kept. They were Turpie, a loveable, clumsy pup with a long gray coat, Balder, who was the image of Spike and would always need extra protection because of his short coat, and Loki, the long-haired, restless, mischievous one.

I learned on my first dogsled trip that the ride wasn't as smooth and relaxing as I had supposed. I also learned that the best-planned, most carefully chosen team became a bedlam of confusion, tangled in traces and towline, when a female malamute was in season. As the team and sled crossed frozen lakes, even though the ice was resilient under the weight, I knew uneasy moments.

A dogteam involved endless work, but, like caring for children, the enjoyment far outweighed the toil.

14. Spring

Spring had come to the north country. One day all had been winter, and the next afternoon, under a bright sun, brown patches appeared on the low hills. Eskimo children roamed the tundra, searching for frozen cranberries, and within a few days, the ice on the bay snapped, cracked, and moved. Ribbons of blue water widened as the ice, lifted by a flood tide, drifted out to the Bering Sea. Three weeks later, following a high tide backed by a strong wind, the river ice broke free. Floes drifted seaward in waters surrounded by snow-covered hills. The sun shone warm and bright, and we had to draw the shades to shut out the glare off the snow.

The lure of the outdoors was strong. Ed, Anecia, and I walked one evening at low tide out on the bay to the edge of the five-foot wall of ice. Ed leaned over the rim, looking below. Suddenly he waved and called to Anecia and me.

"The tide is out so far I can see clams in the mud."

Anecia ran ahead. Just as she reached him, the honeycombed ice gave way, and they both dropped from sight. By the time I reached them, they were scrambling up the crumbling wall.

Another time we hiked over the hills toward the

mouth of the bay. The thick crust would hold us for a few steps, until suddenly we broke through the soft snow to our knees or hips. We envied the light-footed foxes, whose tracks were numerous on the crusted snow.

Ed and I often rose early to hunt ptarmigan. Eager to share with our families what we could of our life in the North, I canned several jars of ptarmigan breasts, and made jam from the little cranberries.

As the snow melted and the days grew longer, ducks and geese returned, and our bay became a nesting ground. The Eskimos often sent us a duck or goose, and one time Pollogen, one of the men of the village, brought us a swan, which we accepted with more regret than gratitude.

Anecia, however, was delighted. Often she had watched her mother prepare the beautiful white skin, carefully turning it inside out and hanging it outside for several days to dry. The large feathers were plucked, leaving down that was as white and soft as a whisper. The skin was tanned and made into parkas for babies, with the down-side in. Preservation of the down was the only comfort I found in the killing of the swan. And that didn't last long. Anecia, while working on the bird outdoors, left it for a moment, and when she returned, the pups had riddled the soft white skin beyond salvage with their teethmarks.

Anecia was both happy and apprehensive about going to work at the hospital at Kanakanak as a nurse's aide. Every few days she wanted reassurance that she could return to us if she were not happy there. One evening at the dinner table she told us that Ocalena had asked her what she would do if the people at the hospital were not good to her.

Anecia looked at Ed. "I tell Ocalena if somebody not good to me, I say to him, 'When Mr. Morgan come I tell him, and when Mrs. Morgan come back from States I come back to Kulukak and live here."

After school was out for the summer, Anecia slept in the classroom. The extra bed we set up there was more comfortable than the narrow couch in the living room. She was happy there until one of the older women frightened her by saying she should never sleep alone in a room that big. Always at night *carayaks* wandered about. So Anecia went to sleep with a light on, and later Ed or I would put it out.

Anecia told us that when a person died at Kulukak or a neighboring village, mothers sprinkled a few drops of water on the heads of their babies and repeated several times the Eskimo name of the deceased, This prevented the children from becoming ill.

For three days following a death in the village, no one used a knife, for fear of cutting the path of the spirit of the deceased. And after a baby was born, the mother skinned no seals for several months. And no one ever glanced in the direction of a grave, but looked the other way while hurrying past it. A deceased person was never referred to by name, except by mothers performing the rite on their babies. A dead person was referred to as "Mollia's dead husband" or "she who has just died."

I wondered how such superstition would mix with hospital routine at Kanakanak. But in Anecia was the understanding of her people as well as the confidence of our people to make for a happy blend in the care of sick Eskimos.

Spike guarded the station with noisy bravado, forcing villagers and travelers to make a cautious approach. But as a hunting dog, he was not so brave. He trotted confidently at Ed's heels the first time they started out ptarmigan hunting, but he soon lost his enthusiasm when Ed fired the shotgun. I looked up to see him tearing over the crest of the hill, gathering speed as he neared the station. He burst into the kitchen with icicles hanging from his chin, and forever after he had a deep distrust of guns. When Ed cleaned the guns in the kitchen, Spike retreated to the bedroom.

One morning I opened the door to find him waiting expectantly, tail wagging and a squirrel in his mouth. He trotted proudly into the living room and waited, like a child eager to be praised, for Ed to take it from him.

"If he'd brought a ptarmigan," Ed said, "I really could forgive him."

Then Spike met with trouble. He'd been romping with the school youngsters and barked at the door to be let in . I opened it and, as he trotted past me, an overpowering smell of rotten fish gagged me. The dog was covered with it. Ed grabbed him by the collar and pulled him back outside. Just then Stephan came around the corner of the house.

"Stephan," Ed inquired, "what happened to Spike?"

"He fall in *tepet* hole."

During the summer, when salmon are running, the villagers put the fish in a hole in the ground, the sides of which are lined with mats woven from beach grass. When the hole is full, it is covered with sticks and grass. In the winter, *tepet* are used for food. In another method of making *tepet*, the salmon heads, rich in oil, are cut open and the sperm sacks, or milt, of the male salmon are placed between layers of the heads. These *tepet* are aged for a month, rinsed of the slime coating, and eaten. The milt is not consumed, as it is added only for the flavor it gives to the heads. Spike, while running with the children, had slipped into the hole containing the thawed remains of last summer's fish.

Ed and I spent a long evening bathing the dog in the washtub in the coal shed. We carried water from the spring, heated it on the range, and carried it to the tub. After a good shampooing and several rinses, Spike still smelled so badly we could scarcely tolerate him near us.

While Ed scrubbed and Spike struggled and the water

splashed, becoming ice after a few moments, Ed remarked that it would have been simpler to have shot him.

Ed worked in the carpenter shack on the little boat he planned to use for fishing. She was twelve feet long and made of what lumber he could find. One May afternoon he put her in the water for the first time, and he, Anecia, and I rowed out to the island for a picnic supper of sandwiches and coffee. We found the island very different from what it had been when we had hiked to it over the ice of the bay. In spring, the low spots were covered with water and seaweed in which herring had laid their eggs.

We came out to the island on the ebb tide and were ready to return to the village before the current changed. Bucking the tide with three people and a dog in the boat was hard work, so Ed let Anecia and me out on the beach, and we hiked home. Anecia stopped beside a rock that stood alone above the water's edge and told me a legend of her people.

Long ago an old grandmother warned her grandsons not to go near the river as ice was going out. The boys disobeyed and played on the ice floes. The current carried them down the river, out into the waters of the bay. Hurriedly, the old grandmother pulled on her red fox-fur parka and ran along the beach, anxiously following and watching the boys as they drifted farther out. When the current carried them out of the bay and into the Bering Sea, and they finally disappeared, she fell hopelessly on a rock, there to remain and grieve. Thereafter, the rock on the shore near Kulukak, red like the fox-fur parka, was believed to be the old woman still waiting for her grandsons.

As we neared the village, Spike came upon a hair seal that had been recently killed by an Eskimo hunter and covered with grass to protect it from the sun. We met Anuska coming to skin it, and watched her begin at the head with her *uluaq* (knife), cutting just under the skin until she had separated the hide from the body as one peels off a sock inside out.

As the time drew near for me to leave for Outside and for Anecia to go to work at the hospital at Kanakanak, we sewed to prepare clothes for her. I gave her everything I could spare, and we altered a blue dress, two skirts, and a coat. When the day came to pack for the trip to Nushagak, more of my clothes were among Anecia's belongings than were in my luggage. I made plans to replenish my wardrobe in the States.

We left sooner than expected. Pollogen had a dangerously infected hand, and Ed was worried about his soaring temperature, the red streaks that crept up his arm, and the ominous swelling. Pollogen had spent hours in our kitchen with his hand and arm in Epsom salt solution, but, in typical Eskimo fashion, appeared less concerned than did Ed.

The morning we were to leave, my trunk already in Peter's sailboat, the wind suddenly shifted.

"Headwind. No travel today," Chris announced. He said the winds had to be right to fill the sails and skim us over the waters of Kulukak Bay, out to the Bering Sea. Now that the time had come to leave, I was torn between eagerness to see Grandmother and the family Outside and love for Ed and this tranquil tundra, now my beloved home.

Chris's launch was at Togiak without gasoline. He had borrowed Peter's sailboat to make the trip for his trading post supplies, planning to take all of us over with him and to bring Ed and Spike back to Kulukak on his return. Pollogen would remain at a village on the river. Our sled dogs were out at the summer camp, where Peter would care for them. Early one morning we finally left Kulukak and made good time until noon, when the sail sagged limply and the boat drifted in calm waters. Whales spouted, and ducks flew past in pairs

close to the surface of the water. The cold gray skies
changed to blue, and our shadow drifted alongside.

Chris sat in the stern, leaning against the gunwale
with his knees tucked under his parka and his fur cap
down over his ears, puffing contentedly on his pipe. He
was completely oblivious to time. Alaska, after all, was
the land of the day after tomorrow.

Pollogen fished off the stern when Ed didn't have him
soaking his hand in Epsom salts in a two-pound coffee
can. He caught a cod and several flounder. The cod is
one of God's ugliest creatures. It has a big, grumpy,
thick-lipped mouth that, even when dead, dares you to
eat him. We watched seals as they watched us, and
porpoises played nearby.

As suddenly as the wind left us, it filled our sails
again and swept us steadily on. We sailed through the
treacherous reefs at Sterling Shoal, rounded Cape Constantine, and made our way through tide rips at Protection Point. Chris handled the sailboat with the same
efficiency and calmness with which he had piloted his
launch when he brought us to Kulukak the previous
fall. Once, when close to shore, he pointed to what
looked like a brick-colored rock on the beach. It was a
dead walrus, washed ashore, perhaps wounded by a
hunter on Walrus Island.

Ed took over the wheel while Chris cut up the cod
and boiled little chunks of it in seawater in a battered
tea kettle.

"See," he said, "it's all salted for you when you do it
this way."

I unpacked sandwiches, dried fruit, and cookies.
Chris jabbed at the boiling fish with a fork.

"Just about ready," he announced. "Then we make
tea in this kettle."

With dusk shortly before midnight, the wind died
again, leaving no alternative but to anchor and lower
sail for the night.

"Might as well sleep as sit," Chris said.

Unmindful of the cold in the open sailboat in early spring, he soon dropped off to sleep in his double-layered squirrelskin parka and fur boots. Pollogen constantly moved about, while Anecia slept in parka and blankets. Ed and I lay in our sleeping bags on a reindeer hide. The night was endless, and I learned how it feels to be so cold you can scarcely keep the tears back.

Daylight came, and with it a headwind. But even that was better than no wind at all. Tacking was tiresome, and our progress was slow. The hours dragged by as we moved over the monotonous gray seas.

We entered the mouth of the Nushagak to find tide as well as wind against us. Chris shook his head.

"Might as well go ashore at Ekuk and wait for the flood tide."

"How long will that be?" I asked.

"Not sure. Maybe four hours."

Chris and Pollogen, with true Eskimo love of visiting, went to the village in search of friends. Ed, Anecia, and I, with Spike, walked up the beach to a cannery. There Anecia saw for the first time a truck, cannery buildings, and tugboat. She stared quietly with amazement at each. As we returned to the village, we saw Chris standing beside a woman who was cleaning the first king salmon caught in the village that spring.

Chris took us to the home of a friend to await the change of tide. There we took off our parkas and fur boots and toasted our feet on a board placed on the open door of a rusted old range. The people played scratchy phonograph records, and we were warm and comfortable.

Suddenly shots rang out, a boat whistled, and the first cannery ship of the spring arrived in the Nushagak River. The shots were the villagers' salute, and the whistle a reply.

Later that day we sailed up the Nushagak and alongside the cannery boat anchored at Clark's Point. Midnight found us in Kanakanak climbing the stairs to the familiar cold, white little bedroom in the girls' dormitory. We left Pollogen at the hospital, where the doctor examined his hand and arm. Chris remained on the boat. At Ted's apartment Anecia saw for the first time a modern bathroom. When Ted asked her to empty coffee grounds in the toilet, she dumped them in the bathtub.

Anecia slept on the floor of our room rather than among strangers in the girls' ward. Through the darkness, I heard her whisper, "Schoolarista, I no can sleep. I see so much. A big ship, an automobile, all these big buildings, upstairs, this kind of button lights, a toilet, and a bathtub. I think I like stay here till you come back from States."

15. No One Home at Kulukak

The engine of the little pontoon plane throbbed.

"Let's get going," the pilot said as he waded over to where I stood with Anecia and a group of our Kanakanak friends.

My eagerly anticipated journey to the States had ended before it began, and I was returning to Kulukak. The day following Ed and Chris's departure, word had reached the radio station of a change in ship schedules that would have left me little time Outside. I wired the family, and they encouraged me to cancel the trip. But I was in Kanakanak with no means of travel back to Kulukak, and I knew it would be fall before Ed and Chris would come back for me. Then news came to the radio station of a plane stopping en route to Bethel (a small city northwest of Kulukak). I made hurried arrangements for the pilot to pick me up and take me home.

With my traveling bag and steamer trunk already on board, the pilot carried me to the plane. He smelled of liquor, and on the floor of the plane I saw an empty whiskey bottle. This was my first plane trip, and I thought that it might well be my last. The pilot introduced me to another passenger, who leaned forward, then sat back straight and tense. He drummed his fingers on his knees. Catching my glance, he pointed to the whiskey flask. I resisted the temptation to ask him if it was his first plane trip, too. He acted just the way I felt.

Then I remembered my last trip from Kanakanak to Kulukak, anchored for days in Ten Day Creek and Mud Lagoon, waiting for an offshore wind, then traveling around Cape Constantine in heavy seas. And I recalled hearing about the heroic rescues and mercy flights of the bush pilots. As it turned out, this plane trip was not so important as what came later.

The propeller was spinning. The plane moved, and I waved good-bye to my friends, wondering when, and if, I would see them again.

The plane taxied over the gray waters of the Nushagak, bouncing as the pontoons slapped the waves. We stopped at a small village where a man waded out and handed a package to the pilot. Then we stopped briefly at Snag Point before heading west to Kulukak. Now that I had canceled my trip Outside, I was eager to get home. It had been hard to say good-bye to Ed, knowing the difficult trip ahead of him and the long, lonely summer.

Flying over the tundra was like looking at a relief map on which the artist had generously used a red-brown color. The country was low and level, cut by sloughs, swamps, lakes, and rivers. There were patches of snow, several herds of reindeer, and, off to our left, the blue water of Bristol Bay and the Bering Sea.

The pilot handled the plane expertly and my nervous fellow passenger ceased drumming his fingers.

"You'll have to direct me," the pilot said. "Never been here before."

After all the months I had lived at the government station atop the hill overlooking Kulukak Bay, I recognized it instantly when we flew near. We entered at the mouth of the bay. Marveling that the trip could not have taken more than fifteen minutes, I pointed in the direction of the station.

"Have to land where there's no rocks. Where would that be?"

I thought rapidly. At low tide rocks were scattered all along the shore, but as the tide was coming in now, I felt certain that a cove a quarter of a mile below the village would be safe. I pointed the pilot toward it.

"We'll circle the house before we land," he teased. "Give him a chance to get the squaws out."

My fellow passenger was again drumming his fingers, and this time I shared his uneasiness. I felt relieved that we hadn't knocked any bricks from the chimney. There was no sign of life below, but Ed couldn't be far and would come as soon as he heard the plane. Spike would be with him.

The pilot set the plane down easily and climbed out. He placed my traveling bag and trunk on the beach near the foot of the cliff. I handed him a check for my fare, and bade my fellow passenger good-bye knowing that he was envious. I was safe, my trip had ended. Looking at the surrounding country, barren and treeless, the pilot muttered, "God, what a place for a white woman to call home."

I was offended. Ed and I had come to love Kulukak, and it surely looked good to me now. He called to the other passenger, asking if he would like to come ashore.

"We'll wait around till your husband comes."

"Oh, no," I said. "He won't be far. Please don't wait."

"I don't like leaving you alone in a place like this."

"There's nothing wrong with this place. I'll be all right."

The pilot told me he would be flying back from Bethel in two days and would stop if he had no passengers.

"If anything should be wrong," he said, "if your husband doesn't show up or you're worried or want to leave, stretch out some white sheets in a T shape and I'll land."

I thanked him and, scarcely waiting for the plane to leave, started up the trail expecting to meet Ed. As I walked through the village, I realized it was completely deserted. Not even a dog was to be seen. Grass grew on some of the sod houses, and one had partly caved in. Every last person was now at the summer fish camp. The only sound that disturbed the silence was the drone of the engine as the airplane disappeared.

From the crest of the hill I saw the roof of the station. No smoke curled from the chimney, and suddenly I had a moment of misgiving. I walked home and was astounded to find the storm door closed. Only when we were away, or during winter storms, was it closed. The back door was just as we had left it. Then I realized that Ed had not yet returned to Kulukak.

I thought of treacherous Cape Constantine, and a deadly fear gripped me.

I dropped on the low step and leaned on the door. The more I thought of the dangers of Ed's journey, the more frightened I became. He and Chris had left Kanakanak a week before in what had seemed favorable weather. Chris had remarked that they would be in Kulukak in a couple of days. I knew that if misfortune had befallen Ed and Chris, most of the summer could go by before I would be able to reach anyone with the news. Would that pilot circle over as he had said he would? Weeks or months could pass before an Eskimo returned to the village.

A light rain made me suddenly remember my trunk and traveling bag. The incoming tide could easily reach them below the cliff. And how would I get into the house? We had so carefully locked the doors and windows, and Ed, wherever he was, had the keys.

I walked down the trail and along the beach, feeling

unspeakably desolate and alone in a very bleak world. I was the only living thing in this deserted village; the nearest Eskimo was at summer fish camp, wherever that was. Togiak and Kanakanak each were days away by water, and I had no boat other than the little skiff. I could do absolutely nothing but wait.

The water had nearly reached my luggage. Unable to get the trunk out of the steep-walled cove, I opened it, took out a dressing gown, tied the sleeves together, and stuffed it full of the things I valued most. Then I dragged the trunk up the beach to the base of the cliff, worked it up to a low shelf, stood it on end, and left it, supposing it would go out with the tide or be beaten by the surf. I made two hurried trips to get the bundle and traveling bag out of the cove.

The increasing drizzle made me anxious to get into the house. I examined all the doors and windows again, hoping desperately that we had forgotten to lock one. We hadn't. The back way was the most encouraging, but it, too, was formidable when I saw the heavy padlock and twenty-penny nails that held the hasp in place. I made several trips to the carpenter shack for tools, first trying to file the padlock, then pounding it with a hammer. Finally, with the hammer claws, I went after the twenty-penny nails. After what seemed like hours, the two-by-four cross boards finally loosened, and I pulled out the last stubborn nail.

The house was quiet and cold, and I was uneasy at remaining alone indefinitely. I took the clock off the shelf and wound it. I didn't know the time because my watch was on its way to the States for repair, but the next day, if the sun shone, I could get an approximation. At noon the sun would cast a shadow from a window bar that coincided with a line Ed had made on the floor for just such an emergency. I guessed at the time and felt easier when the clock ticked.

I brought in my things and built a fire in the range.

Kulukak in winter, showing *barabaras*, fish caches, and the bay.

Just to keep busy, I prepared a lunch I wasn't able to eat. I bathed, then went to bed. But remaining in bed with my thoughts was intolerable, and sleep was impossible. I got up and dressed.

Some time during the night I sat by the window and hemmed a skirt. As I sipped scalding coffee, I wondered if I should try to find the nearest summer camp and send someone to look for Ed and Chris. A new thought tormented me. If their boat had gone down, and they managed to reach shore in the kayak that was always in tow of the sailboat, there would be miles of beach and swamp to traverse before they could reach Kulukak Bay. Should I fire a gun in the hope that someone might hear the shots and come?

I knew there was no help in becoming panicky or terror-stricken. What I must face, I could. All I could do was wait, and wait.

For perhaps the thousandth time, I stood at the window overlooking the bay. Suddenly a sailboat drifted silently into sight. I had looked so often, I could not believe what I was seeing. I watched her, hardly daring to hope Ed would be on board. But as the sailboat approached, I grew more certain it was Peter's. There was a fair wind, and the boat was making good time. Then she disappeared behind the hill.

I set my cup on the desk and ran outside. In a few minutes Spike came running up the trail. Ed was not far behind. He was unshaven, weary, and dirty. I stood there too happy to speak.

Then Ed saw me. He stopped dead in his tracks, and I knew he didn't quite believe his eyes. After a moment, he managed the heartfelt welcome, "Just how in hell did you get back here?"

Over breakfast, which I prepared while Ed bathed in the washtub in the middle of the kitchen floor, we had a great deal to tell each other. The wind had changed a few hours after he and Chris left Kanakanak, and they were forced to spend days at anchor in a cove awaiting an offshore wind before attempting the trip around the cape. They ate only pilot bread, soggy crackers, and sardines, and they spent hours walking along the beach.

As they approached Kulukak, they had seen what looked like a box or chest on a shelf in the cove, and Ed planned to investigate later. So I still had my trunk. Chris had left immediately for the summer seal camp.

The clock ticked, the fire crackled, and Spike walked over to me and put his head on my lap. Ed helped himself to another hotcake. All was well with my world.

16. The *North Star*

The waters of Kulukak Bay were smooth as the sun dropped from sight. Blue sky, fleecy white clouds, and the hills surrounding the little bay were reflected in its depths. The ship, a phantomlike vessel, was outlined on the horizon beyond the mouth of the bay.

"We should have started an hour ago," Ed remarked as he gave me a hand into a skiff. "Then rowing would have been easy all the way."

He settled himself comfortably and adjusted the oars.

"The tide is ebbing, but in a couple of hours, at the most, it will change. If we haven't reached the ship by then, we'll have to buck the current."

The evening was clear and quiet. The only sound was of the oars cutting the water and of the rhythmic grinding of the oarlocks. With long, regular strokes, Ed pulled the boat swiftly.

The government supply ship *North Star* called at our station once a year, and now she was anchored outside the bay, awaiting the flood tide so her launch and lighter could enter the shallow water of the channel to bring our year's provisions to the beach. For weeks we had been without coal and many staples such as flour, potatoes, bacon, and coffee. Soon we would have fresh

The *North Star*

fruit and vegetables and, perhaps, fresh meat other than reindeer. But above all, we would see and talk with people from Outside. We were more eager for that than for any of the supplies. Many weeks had passed since we had seen anyone from the States, and as the days grew longer, radio reception had become weaker, until finally the radio was silent.

"We're beginning to buck the tide," Ed remarked as we neared the little island that stood halfway between the village and the mouth of the bay. The current, instead of carrying us along, now flowed against us. A strong headwind blew up as we left the harbor and entered the open waters of the Bering Sea. The sky darkened, and the water heaved with heavy swells. The shore looked very far away.

"Hadn't we better turn back?" I said.

"The ship is closer now than the station."

"But she's still far away, and in open sea."

"Wouldn't you like to see the supply ship, talk with the officers, and hear news from Outside? If we don't go out, we'll see them only for the little time it takes to unload the lighter."

Ed rowed tirelessly with long, steady strokes. The skiff, just twelve feet long, began to take on water, and I bailed with a coffee can. We shot down into a trough and were lifted up and over a crest, then swept down again. Sometimes we could see the ship, and sometimes she was lost to us by the high walls of gray water and sky.

Back at the village, we had thought the ship to be within four miles. Already we had come six or seven. Water distance, we realized, could be extremely deceiving.

I had a mighty respect and deep-rooted fear of the Bering Sea. Ed's jaws were set hard, and he was rowing with all his strength. The bailing went on and on, but water was ankle deep in the skiff. Ed turned to glance at the ship, and I anxiously watched the now-indistinct coastline. Gradually, the distance between us and the ship lessened. She appeared motionless, secure, and confident in the rough waters.

At last we came abreast of her. People stood on the deck, and Ed rowed toward the stern. As we reached the waters to the lee of the vessel, the swells were cut through by return swells that had slapped the ship's side. Slowly, Ed circled the stern, and then, scarcely using his oars, he let the tide and wind carry us alongside. A Jacob's ladder came down, and from the deck someone shouted, "Come up the ladder. Let your boat go."

I stared at the ladder. One minute it was ten or twelve feet above the water, and the next, as a giant swell swept past, it dipped down into the sea. It lay against the ship's gray side, then, as the ship rolled, it swung out over the water. I watched with terror.

"Ed, I can't go up the ladder! I can't!"

"You haven't any choice."

He guided the skiff carefully, timing her movements to the ship's roll.

"Take off your gloves and be ready."

"I can't!"

"Quick, now. Grab it and hang on."

Terrified, I reached for it, and I hung on. Then Ed was beside me.

"Climb!" he shouted.

Afraid to move or release my grip, I clung to the ropes.

"Climb, hurry!"

I couldn't move.

"Climb! We'll be in ice water in another minute. Don't look down!"

Ed's fingers were a vise on my arm, pushing me. We pulled ourselves up a few rungs, swung out over the water, and then slapped against the ship's side. Slowly, carefully, we made our way up the rope ladder. Helping hands reached from above as we neared the top. Friendly faces, blurred to me, welcomed us. Ed shook hands, but I stood gripping the rail and staring at the water below. The skiff, tossing lightly and aimlessly, was a mere toy in the heaving sea.

A voice from beside me said, "Are you anxious about your boat? Some of the crew will go after her."

I shook my head and didn't say that right then I hoped never to see that skiff again.

One of the officers slipped binoculars into a case and said, "We've been watching you for some time and were about ready to come after you."

To our surprise, Mrs. Schrammeck and Wallace, completely recovered from his illness, were on board. For several pleasant hours we sat around the table in the ship's social hall and enjoyed coffee and conversation with Captain Whitlam, three government officials who were on an inspection tour of the schools, Mrs. Schrammeck, and the ship's officers. Then, in the half-light of the Alaska dawn, we climbed down the Jacob's ladder into the launch that had been lowered over the ship's side. The lighter, laden with our provisions, and the skiff, which the crew had recovered, were in tow.

Captain Whitlam, the government men, several of the ship's officers, Ed, and I rode in the launch. The crew members perched on boxes of our provisions. Clowning and full of fun, two of the sailors made the trip in our skiff, towed behind the lighter.

When we reached our beach, a heavy mist and the chill of early morning hurried us up to the station while the crew unloaded the barge. Opening the door, we were greeted by the aroma of the bread I had taken from the oven shortly before we left for the ship.

"Mm, fresh bread," one of the government inspectors said. "And stoves that are polished. What a cozy, attractive home."

After a brief inspection of the station and classroom, the men settled with us in the living room to discuss the reports, the reindeer work, and the new warehouse to be constructed near the beach. One of the men from the Juneau office asked about Anecia.

"Are you planning to bring her back to Kulukak this fall?"

We said that we felt it would be better if she did not return to the village.

The inspector said, "She received her appointment as a government employee, and the doctor would like to keep her at the hospital, but she told him she's coming back here to live with you people."

"We took her to Kanakanak because she was very

unhappy in the village, and Mrs. Morgan planned to be gone all summer," Ed said. "She went with our assurance she could always come back if she wanted to."

"She's a most superior worker, very capable, very good at interpreting," the man said. "The hospital staff would like you to influence her to remain."

"We'll do what we can," Ed promised. "Perhaps a visit would satisfy what might be a touch of homesickness."

We were interrupted by a knock at the door. On the porch, holding a box from which celery stalks peeked out, was a member of the ship's crew. Roses could not have been a more welcome sight than those celery leaves.

"Captain sent this. We'll have the unloading done in an hour."

The men wanted to visit an Eskimo dwelling, so we took them to Wassilia's *barabara*. A sleepy family stirred from their bunks at Ed's call in the tunnel entrance. They smiled their welcome as we introduced our visitors from the ship. Ed then showed the men the *qasgiq* while I waited on the beach. Of the fish Ed had taken from his net the night before, he put a dozen on the lighter for future dinners aboard ship.

With the turn of the tide, the launch and barge pulled away, and we watched our visitors disappear in the heavy mist. Ed and I stood shivering near the water's edge beside the mountain of boxes, crates, lumber, and sacks of coal. Wearily, Ed looked at the pile of provisions.

"The flour and sugar are together here," he said. "Think I'll get them up to the station right away because of this drizzle. I can cover the rest with tarps. Some of the heavier boxes will have to stay till the men return from fishing and can help me."

At noon, while we enjoyed fresh grapefruit for the first time in many months, there was a commotion in the back yard. There we found women and children,

THE *NORTH STAR* 141

smiling proudly, and laden with boxes of our supplies. Ed and I pitched in, and before bedtime everything except the heaviest crates, sacks of coal, and lumber for the warehouse was up from the beach. The people of the village were eager to help, and they happily hurried down the hill for load after load. What had seemed a terrific task to Ed and me was turned into a gala occasion by the eager hands of our friends. At day's end we gave them packages of tea, bars of soap, tins of fruit, and bars of candy.

Among the provisions were anxiously awaited boxes of books, medicines, school supplies, gasoline for lamps, groceries, and dogteam and sled equipment. Remaining on the beach was a new range to replace the old one with its broken draft window that spilled ashes and its saggy, uneven top that blackened all the kettles.

At low tide the next afternoon, Ed pulled on his boots in preparation for his trip to his fishnet.

"You'd better stay in the house," he told me. "It's beginning to rain, and the mosquitoes are thick."

As I finished the dishes, I glanced out at the backyard. Corrugated boxes were torn to bits, and pieces of wood from the crates were scattered about. The pups, Ed's embryo dogteam, had had themselves a romp. Every box was precious and before winter would be reduced to kindling and piled neatly in the coal shed.

I slipped into rain clothes and began to clean up the mess. The pups, eager to play, tugged at whatever I picked up. Suddenly I heard a strange drawing sound that reminded me of fire with the dampers open pulling a strong draft. The thought was terrifying. I dropped my load and listened. The sound came from inside the house. I dashed to the back door and into the kitchen. The far end of the room was in flames.

"No," I thought. "This house can't burn. No other shelter, no other protection, no other place to go."

I thought of the year's provisions, the medicines, all

of the food, and the dry lumber stored in the attic. If the flames reached there, it would be lost. Quickly, with a pounding heart, I shut the door behind me, covered my head with my coat and ran to the far end of the room to close the living room door. Choking, and eyes smarting from the smoke, I snatched the fire extinguisher and frantically tried to pump it. The handle jammed. With a sob of despair, I threw it aside and grabbed a pail. Just outside the kitchen door, in the coal shed, Ed kept a wash boiler full of water. I filled the pail again and again, dashing water on the fire.

The flames died. Clouds of white smoke rolled up in ribbons from the woodwork. Tears nearly blinded me. Sparks glowed red and smoldered in the wood. The fire had started on the floor at the base of the corner cupboard by the range. The trap door in the ceiling was blistered and charred. Standing on a chair, I dashed more water on it, anxious about the lumber stored just above.

Hurrying through the living room and hall and into the schoolroom, I pulled the bell rope. Ed would come the instant he heard it.

Still uneasy that a spark might flare into flames, I returned to the kitchen and listened for any sound of fire from the attic. My tidy, attractive kitchen was streaked with water and smoke. The door leading to the living room was scorched, the woodwork of the corner cupboard was burned crisp, and the floor was a lake of water and soot.

I went outside, sat on a box in the yard, and shed bitter tears. A long, long time later, Ed came around the corner of the house, whistling gaily, the pups racing around him. I then realized the wind was from the west, and he hadn't heard the bell. He stopped suddenly.

"What's the matter?"

I pointed toward the house.

He went inside, and there was another whistle, a

long, drawnout exclamation, very different from the one
that had announced his arrival a few minutes before.

He came out, seated himself on a box, and pushed his
cap back on his head.

"Know how it started?"

I shook my head. "Must have been a spark from the
draft on the side of the stove.

"Scare you?"

"What do you think?"

I shed more tears.

The next day Wassilia became the happy recipient of
the old range. A flying spark could do no harm to the
sod floor of his *barabara*. Removing the legs, Ed helped
him maneuver it through the tunnel and low doorways
of his dwelling. They set it up, replacing the oil drum
that had served as a stove. Wassilia was as delighted
with his range as I was with mine.

17. Summer

Summer was an industrious time, and long days allowed us to accomplish much. Ed's plans seemed enough to fill two summers. He wanted to catch two thousand salmon for dog food and build a small warehouse where supplies could be stored from the unloading of the supply ship in the spring until the snow was deep enough to haul them with a dogsled. He also wanted to build a springhouse with a trapdoor in the roof so we could more easily obtain water when snow drifts were deep, and a smokehouse in which to cure salmon. And before winter set in he had to round up the reindeer and build a dogsled. Despite daily interruptions, he accomplished it all.

He placed his salmon net a half mile below the village. On June 4 he caught the first fish—six red salmon and thirty-seven flounder. The next day he caught fifty-two salmon, six flounder, and one duck. There were times when as many as seventy-five salmon hung in the net as the tide receded. Near the beach, on a makeshift table with a nail driven up through the top to hold the fish from slipping, Ed prepared his salmon for drying. After removing the head and entrails, he slit down both sides of the backbone, removing it without

144

severing the body from the tail. After two diagonal slashes were cut across the sides, two backs were tied together with string and hung over a pole to dry. A rack, high enough to be out of the reach of the dogs, located at the top of the bluff, supported the poles where fish dried in the sun before going into the smokehouse. A gasoline drum placed on its side served as the smokehouse stove. The task of rowing to the net, picking out the fish, rowing back to the village, and preparing the fish for the racks took hours. Millions of mosquitoes swarmed where Ed worked. He insisted that no fish entrails be left lying around the village because of the big blackflies. Seagulls were another annoyance as they brazenly carried away fish from the racks. When the net was taken in in late August, 2,154 fish hung in the smokehouse.

The day the villagers returned from their summer seal camps, Ed gave all of them salmon.

"Peter," he called, "tell them to take fish from my nets until theirs are up."

But they never did so without asking. Evon got us out of bed early one morning. Holding up three fingers, he said, "Me take fish."

The villagers often refused offers of fish, but they gratefully accepted heads and eggs. The heads were rich in oil, and they were packed into inflated seal stomachs along with the dried dark red eggs. Seal oil was poured around them, and the poke tightly closed and hung to dry. Later it was sliced thin for eating.

One day as I walked through the village, I came upon Chris standing by Anuska, who squatted in the grass cleaning salmon. He chewed on something crunchy, which sounded like celery. Chris spoke to Anuska in Yup'ik, and with her *uluaq* she cut a strip from the back of the fish and a piece from what corresponded to the forehead. Smilingly, she held it out to me.

"Eat it, Schoolarista. It's good," Chris said.

Fish rack with one thousand red salmon, drying before going to the smokehouse. The fish were to be winter feed for our dogteam. Twice a day we would pick the salmon from our net, slit them lengthwise, and hang them over the rack, tail fins up.

I looked at the piece of raw fish. Chris waited, and I shook my head.

"I can't, Chris."

Laughingly, he took it, and in accompaniment to the celery-crunching sound, said, "Too bad, Schoolarista. Too civilized."

One day the sleepy little village suddenly became a busy shipping port with sailboats moving in and out of the bay, bringing back families, dogs, and supplies. The beach was littered with the fruits of their work, and no port could have boasted more interesting cargo than that unloaded on our beach that day.

There were seal stomachs full of oil, bundles of dried squirrel skins tied together at the necks, dried herring, halibut, cod, and flounder. There were parchmentlike rolls of dried seal and walrus gut to be made into rain-wear. There were stacks of duck, squirrel, and muskrat skin for parkas. There were bundles of rolled-up seal and walrus skins for mukluks, kayaks, and rawhide.

Rawhide cutting was a fascinating procedure. The hide had been cured with urine, and all the hair removed. A man using his finger for a gauge cut with a sharp knife around and around until the pelt was one long strip of rawhide that was then stretched out in the sun to complete the curing.

There were chunks of dried meat—seal, walrus, and beluga whale. And there was fresh walrus meat. The skin was reddish-brown in color and wrinkled. Between the skin and a layer of fat was tough, elastic flesh, perhaps four inches thick. Boiled walrus was considered a delicacy.

The resourceful Eskimos even made use of the walrus teeth, fastening two on each side of their kayaks near the opening to hold spears. Also from the walrus, they obtained a muscle fibre used by the women for thread in making mukluks, rainwear, and the covering of kayaks. A cord found in the back of the reindeer was used similarly.

On the beach was a pile of walrus tusks, the root ends bloody and jagged. Some of these would be taken to the trading post, and others were carved into trinkets, snow knives for the children, or lures in smelt fishing.

There were pokes containing dried, smoked herring in seal oil. The men took these, along with the oil-filled pokes, by dogsled to the marsh north of the station. There they buried them in a hole under cold water and concealed them with brush.

Most colorful of all were the baskets and boxes of eggs taken from the cliffs on Walrus Island and from lakes and marshes. The large, speckled murre eggs, in a variety of sizes, were especially beautiful, ranging in color from white to green, blue, and gray. Nature protected

Murre eggs. The Eskimos went out to the islands and robbed the nests in the spring.

them by making one end pointed, causing them to roll in a small circle when moved or pushed, thus being unlikely to fall off a narrow ledge.

Sophia brought us a basket of murre eggs. The shells were thick and hard, and the flavor of the rich gold yokes was remarkably strong.

Also intriguing were the bundles of dried herring eggs covered with grass mats. In the spring, herring lay their eggs in seaweed near the surface of the water.

Gathered by the Eskimos, the clear eggs were spread on the grass to dry, then wrapped in mats woven from beach grass. They were stored in the fish caches and during the dark winter, before being eaten, were soaked in water, then dipped in seal oil. The Eskimos also enjoyed herring eggs just as they came from the water when first gathered.

Hardly had the people returned from the summer camp when the men prepared to leave for Nushagak to fish for the canneries. A sailboat from Cape Pierce stopped at Kulukak, and one of the men, suffering from three crushed fingers, came to the station for medical help. On the twenty-eight-foot boat were twenty-two Eskimos—men, women, and children—and seven dogs. They, with the men from our village, left early one morning for the trip around the cape. Peter took our mail and a letter to Cousin Edgar, inviting him to come back with Peter after the fishing season.

While the men fished on the Nushagak, the women fished at home for salmon to dry for winter. Our beach was lined with set nets, which were full of fish as the tides ebbed.

And as I gathered violets and iris as lovely as those found in any florist's shop Outside, the villagers gathered food from the tundra meadows. Young, curled bracken fronds with their roots were taken home to be boiled, and there were wild greens similar to our celery and spinach. From the marshes the women pulled a broad-bladed grass with an onionlike white root, which was eaten raw. At the edges of lakes, where the women waded to a depth of a couple of feet, they picked an asparaguslike shoot that grew a foot above the water.

Toward the end of July the men of Kulukak sailed back into the harbor. Peter handed us two letters from Edgar. With excitement—and disappointment—we read them. He was on the Nushagak during the fishing season, but we wouldn't see him. If he had come to

Kulukak with Peter, he would have had no way of getting back to Nushagak before the cannery ships returned to the States. He could go without charge on one of the boats from the cannery where he worked. His plan was to return to college in the fall.

Poignant and delightful messages came from Anecia. During a spell of homesickness, she wrote, "I sure was missed when you left. Every time I sit down to eat, I lost my appetite because I so lonely." Then she told us, "There two cows here now. That other one that just come on boat, they call him a bull cow."

It was like Christmas opening our packages from home. We received clothes the family had picked out for us and a pair of binoculars that eclipsed all else for Ed. There were boxes and boxes of books, as well as oranges, apples, cabbages, and watermelon sent from the store at Dillingham.

In late summer the tundra abounded in berries, the most common of which was the little cranberry. Just before freezing time, the Eskimos went in search of mouse holes, which they worked with their feet, feeling for a hollow place. From there, they dug to the rodent's storehouse, taking little roots half the size of a thumbnail. After being boiled, the roots were a sweet delicacy. Ocalena said that sometimes the root was added to *akutaq,* the mixture of melted reindeer tallow and seal oil beat up with snow, sugar, and berries.

One morning that summer Evon awakened Ed early, calling, "*Taitai,* Chunook."

Chunook was the *tyone*'s small daughter, a first grader. Ed and I dressed and hurried down to the village.

Nachuk, the *tyone*'s wife, walked back and forth at the entrance to the *barabara,* sobbing. We found Chunook in the throes of a convulsion, stretched out on the bunk, her body twitching, her head in her father's lap. The *tyone*'s head was bent, and his tears fell on the

The Tyone's wife Olga with son Madfy and daughter Alexia

child's face. Ed slipped a pencil from his pocket between the child's gnashing teeth, and motioned the *tyone* to hold it there.

Evon looked at Ed. "Chunook die?"

"Chunook will be all right."

Evon shook his head. "*Assiituq* [bad]. *Assiituq*."

Ocalena came into the dwelling, and Ed spoke immediately to her.

"Ocalena, tell them Chunook will be all right in a little while." He pointed to the tunnel entrance. "Tell Nachuk, too."

After the seizure subsided, Chunook dropped into a deep sleep. Ed and I left, but returned often that day. During the afternoon Evon came running up to the station.

"Chunook all right! Chunook all right!" he shouted.

Ed and I went down and found the *tyone* on the bunk, his arm around Chunook. Several times while we were there, he put both arms around her, chattered to her, and smiled. Later, I took Chunook some hot soup, and the *tyone* put the dish on his knees, picked up the spoon, and fed her.

"Ocalena," I said, "tell him it might be too hot for her."

The *tyone* stuck his finger in the soup, then nodded to me that it was just right, and began feeding Chunook.

Ocalena and I walked back to the station. "Long time ago *tyone*'s sister die when she sick just like Chunook. *Tyone* and Nachuk scared Chunook die."

When school started a few days later, I was startled to find the *tyone* among the students. Chunook, pale and timid, clung to her father. Suddenly she sobbed, saying there were balls of fire in front of her. The *tyone* shook his head when we urged him to take her to the doctor. During the school day, he sat on one of the low benches at the reading table, keenly interested in all that went on. I gave him magazines and a catalog. As he thumbed through the pages of the big mail-order book, he suddenly broke into laughter, jumped up, and nudged Charlie and Ilutsik. They all giggled, and I saw that the *tyone* was pointing to illustrations of women modeling corsets.

After the men returned from fishing, bringing the ingredients for the *piivaq* barrel, the drinking increased. Often, the girls and many of the women came to the station to spend the night on reindeer hides in the schoolroom. Ed kept a slow fire for them.

When Lucy came one day to have her boils dressed, her jovial, teasing, inebriated uncle followed her. Unable to understand what he wanted, I called Ocalena to act as interpreter. Lucy's uncle wanted to see her boils, and Lucy had no intention of displaying the afflicted part of her anatomy. Ed was down at the warehouse, and Lucy's uncle wouldn't leave. Finally, Lucy pulled up her skirt, showing him the lowest boil just above her knee. He nodded, satisfied, then went over and settled himself in one of the school seats. He pounded the desk and cried, "Schoolarista! Schoolarista!"

About this time, Ed walked in and pointed the uncle toward the door. He asked Lucy to remind him that no one who had been drinking was to come to the station. The uncle shouted laughingly, "Give me hell. Give me hell," and went down the trail. As far as we knew, those three words were the extent of his English vocabulary.

Ed's last task of the summer was the reindeer roundup, at which the herders worked for weeks from dawn until dark. A mile from the village they built a corral of willow brush, and then combed the tundra for miles around searching for deer. When satisfied that all the reindeer were rounded up, the men worked in the corral to count, mark and castrate the animals. It was grueling work, and Ed returned home at dark tired, dirty, and hungry.

Quietly, so as not to excite the animals and separate

does from fawns, small bands were taken from the herd and driven to the corral. The older deer coughed and panted, while the fawns grunted and the does called in deep tones.

To Ed's annoyance, the people of Kulukak found fun in everything. Despite efforts to keep the work quiet and gestures at a minimum, the people couldn't resist the temptation of aiming a freshly removed reindeer testis at an unsuspecting comrade. Twice this frightened the deer and sent them through the brush enclosure. Where one reindeer went, others surely followed.

After the deer were driven into the corral, they milled about for some time before quieting down. In the first excitement, one deer fell, broke its leg, and had to be killed. At the end of the day, the Eskimos butchered the animal and ate the raw heart. Ocalena told us that not all the flesh was eaten raw, only the heart, stomach lining, a stringy muscle that runs down the back of the leg, and the tallow—either warm or cold.

After the roundup, it was with relief that Ed transferred the information from torn and bloodstained tally sheets to the records to be sent to Nome.

18. Salvage

The launch plowed steadily through the cold blue water with Ed at the wheel. She rode deep in the water, her ballast increased by the weight of our winter provisions stowed in her hold. Peter sat on the low cabin and puffed his pipe contentedly, while Spike was lost in sleep. Secured to the stern, our skiff skimmed the water as lightly as a kayak. All was quiet except for the throb of the engine. I only hoped it would continue to throb. There were times when it hadn't.

"This weather won't last," Peter said. "Maybe we'll make it around the cape before she changes, maybe not."

Alaska, the land of day after tomorrow. Regardless of urgency, you waited on winds, tides, and weather.

"Better get in toward shore, Ed. Sand bars ahead and shallow water."

"Look," Ed pointed, "there's a boat in the shadow of that highest cliff. She's been washed up on the beach."

A few moments later, Peter dropped the anchor of the launch, and the men climbed into the skiff and rowed to shore. Upright in the dry sand, parallel to the water's edge and not far from its reach, was a sailboat. Spike and I watched the men examine her inside and out.

Spike, with an air of expectancy, sat on his haunches and wagged his tail hopefully. He was eager to race along the beach to chase seagulls.

A sudden gust of wind whipped us. Peter had said this favorable weather would not last. Why couldn't they have found this boat on the other side of the cape? Ed rowed back.

"That boat's worth salvaging," he said. "She's a good size and isn't damaged. Peter thinks she'll float on the flood tide coming before long. How about coming ashore? It's a nice beach for a walk."

The hull of the beached sailboat had once been red, but now the paint was blistered and peeled. The mast, oars, and boom lay inside the hull, and in the hold was rock ballast. The boat was complete except for an anchor, and that was the reason she lay there. During a storm a few days before, she had broken away from her moorings. The frayed line dangled from the hull, and winds and tide had driven her onto the beach.

"It's hard to tell where she came from," Peter said. "Maybe Nushagak, maybe Naknek. In this country, a lost boat belongs to the finder."

"But how can we take her back to Kulukak?" I asked.

To my horror and dismay, I learned that the men planned to tow the boat around the cape. In my opinion, one boat washed up on the beach was preferable to two in those waters.

We strolled along the beach and waited for the flood tide.

"What will you do with the boat if you get her to Kulukak?" I asked.

Peter puffed his pipe and thought. "Maybe the man who lost her will come look for her."

He'd never come to Kulukak, I thought. Nobody came beyond the treacherous waters of the cape—nobody but the Eskimos who lived at Kulukak or Togiak and the government teachers who traveled with Peter or Chris.

Even the greenest cheechako knew enough to keep away.

"Can always use an extra fishing boat," he added.

At high tide, waves lapped the beach three feet from the boat. I rejoiced, knowing we would get around the cape that night before the weather changed.

"Tide won't come any higher," Peter said. "We might as well be on our way."

Ed walked around the sailboat, eyeing her apprehensively from all directions.

"Peter," he shouted, "what do you say we try to float her? Let's throw out this ballast, pry up the hull, slide the oars, mast, and boom under her, and roll her down to the water."

Together, we pried, pushed, and pulled. Peter said without hope, "It can't be done. We need a couple more men."

Then, with just two feet to go to the water, we tried again. My hands were covered with wet sand, my cap and mittens bulged from my coat pockets, and my slacks were wet and muddy, but finally the sailboat was afloat.

"Tough job for two and a half men," Peter said with a smile.

We turned the launch toward the village, now towing two boats, and darkness was closing over us. It was then that Peter said the words that I knew would come sooner or later.

"We anchor tonight in Mud Lagoon."

Anchor tonight, and maybe tomorrow night, and the next after that. I knew it was madness to attempt the cape in the dark with a storm blowing up out of the west and two boats in tow. A sense of security, for at least this night, settled over me as the anchor dropped in the waters of the lonely creek.

Our meal that evening consisted of cold sandwiches. The only light shone from the Coleman lantern that swung from the cabin ceiling in rhythm with the boat's roll. Our chairs were potato crates, and our tea was brewed in the same battered kettle that Chris had used to boil cod over the little gasoline stove.

All night the salvaged boat restlessly tugged at her mooring line and banged against the launch as wind and waves lashed her. With a thunderous sound, the anchor dragged. In my wakefulness, there was dread of the next day's journey.

Daylight and flood tide brought water so rough we were forced to fight our way out of the "crab seas" of Mud Lagoon. Light and empty, except for the skiff the men had stowed in the hold, the sailboat lurched and tugged with rebellion. The water was a rushing mass of whitecaps that held us back. With terror I watched the men battle the onrushing current. We waited tense moments with the anchor raised and the engine running. Then, with a lull in the current, Peter opened the throttle, and we dashed for open water.

Storm clouds were dark and heavy. As each swell lifted us, the propeller raced above the water. Then a wave washed over the deck and, with a lurch, the sailboat broke away.

"Damn her," Peter shouted.

"Don't turn now," Ed yelled back. "Tide rip. Hold 'er steady."

For the moment, I was glad we were rid of the sailboat, but then I realized she had carried off our skiff. Carefully, Peter turned the launch, and the raw, strong wind whipped us. Water washed over the gunwales, and sea spray blew high and dense. Ed secured Spike to the mast.

Peter's next words to Ed left me cold with fear.

"We'll go alongside. You grab the rope."

Ed braced himself and leaned over the side. The frayed rope dangled tauntingly as Peter steered closer. The sailboat lunged, and we were past, the line beyond Ed's reach. Again Peter turned the launch toward the sailboat, which leaped and careened like a paper in a whirlwind.

"Here we go!" Peter shouted.

Then, without warning, the engine died. Peter mumbled something I couldn't hear, and Ed, keeping his eyes on the sailboat, took the wheel.

With the engine quiet, the turbulent gray seas and dark skies enveloped us. Seals bobbed about as we wallowed aimlessly in the waves. One little head, looking wise and sure of himself, popped out of the water near the stern of the launch, and for the moment diverted Ed's attention.

"He's laughing at us," I said. "He's thinking what fools mortals be."

Ed's answer was a crooked grin.

Peter's head appeared at the hatch.

"Damned if I know what's the matter with this engine!"

Ed disappeared into the cabin while I held the wheel. The voices of the two men were impatient, and I could hear Peter say that we had no time to lose, for the wind and tide soon would force the launch onto the shoals, and our skiff was floating farther away by the moment.

The seas grew higher and the troughs deeper.

"Can you see the sailboat?" Ed called from below deck.

"Yes!" I shouted. "I can right now!"

I knew Ed would never let the sailboat go, now that the skiff was in her. As the giant swells tossed the boat, she would be lost from sight, then suddenly her bow would rise as she pitched on a high crest.

Peter appeared on deck, took bearings from the coastline, scanned the dark skies, then disappeared again below. Tales of boats lost on the reefs off the cape, of the treacherous shoals that claimed the lives of fishermen, and of the intensely cold water pulled at my thoughts.

Then the engine started, only to die again after a few uncertain throbs. Again it turned, throbbed, stopped. Peter, with increased anxiety, darted to the hatch and scanned the distant shore. I knew by his behavior that we were dangerously close to the shoals.

The roll from the swells was now so heavy that our boxes and crates shifted with the boat's motion. I thought of the tale I had heard of a pair of teachers who, caught in the bay by storms and changing winds one fall, had been forced to jettison much of their winter provisions.

Ed came to the hatch, gave me a quick glance, and smiled with confidence. His calmness reassured me.

As the men worked frantically below deck, I heard Ed ask Peter, "How far are we from the shoals?"

"Don't know for sure. Never been this close. But we're too close, I know that."

Suddenly a flash of lightning cut the skies, followed by a crash of thunder. Lightning made jagged live wires all around us, and one crash of thunder followed another. Spike barked and pulled to free himself from the mast. I couldn't tell from which direction the wind was coming, and the shoreline was lost in the fury of the storm.

Peter dashed up, glanced searchingly at the skies and water, then disappeared below.

"My God!" I heard him say. "We must be nearly on the shoals!"

Then I heard Ed say, "Try her now, Peter."

The engine turned a half-hearted sputter while I held my breath. It started again, only to die. Peter tried once more, and this time the irregular pulsations settled into a definite rhythm. We headed straight out to the Bering Sea, and my heart began to beat again.

Gradually, the storm moved on. Peter got out his pipe and stuck it into his mouth. "We must have drifted a half mile," he said.

Then Ed mentioned the sailboat.

Nobody answered when I implored, "Let 'er go. Please let 'er go."

But later Ed was insistent, saying, "We have to get the skiff if we can."

The men peered in the direction we had last seen the sailboat, and for what seemed like hours in that rough water, we cruised and searched. My spirits sank steadily. I knew that Ed and Peter, driven by the will to conquer and subdue, would search until they recovered the sailboat.

Their faces shone wet and ruddy from the rain and spray, and the bitter wind continued to lash us.

Then Peter pointed straight ahead as the bow of the sailboat rose over a crest. Ed moved to the port gunwale and made ready to snatch the rope as Peter sidled the launch over. I thought surely that Ed could never hold that careening, wild boat, that he would be pulled overboard. The launch moved closer, and then the boats collided with a thunderous jolt as they were caught in a downsweep and rushed into a trough.

"Got her!" Ed shouted, and with desperation he clung to the rope and the gunwale while the sailboat plunged and pulled like an unbroken mustang.

Peter shouted, "Schoolarista, here, take the wheel. Hold 'er steady."

I flew to Peter's side, and he ran to help Ed hold the rope. Timing their movements to the sweep of the seas, the men secured lines to the sailboat.

"Now she'll hold," Peter said. "These lines could tow a freighter."

The men turned back to the work of handling the launch. Peter, with the hint of a swagger, took the wheel while Ed rubbed his rope-burned hands.

Peter considered the skies and water, then said, "We can't make it around the cape in this. Think we better head back to Ten Day Creek for tonight."

But there, too, we found giant rollers breaking at the mouth of the creek. Peter turned the launch and headed back to seek shelter at the first place possible. Despite heavy seas, we made it into Protection Point Lagoon just at dark.

The following morning, while waiting for the flood tide, we explored the beach and picked up driftwood to load into the salvaged sailboat. It would make precious firewood. Snow had capped the mountains during the night, and a fresh, clean, cold breeze blew in from the Bering Sea, filling me with the sheer joy of living. As I walked along the water's edge, I felt calm, content, and near to God in the beauty and serenity of that remote world. With the tranquility of dawn, the fears and terror of the day before were gone.

Toward evening, the launch entered the waters of Kulukak Bay. The men decided to give the salvaged boat to the *tyone,* who could use her to fish on the river for the canneries.

"Is that OK with you?" they asked, recognizing my half-man interest.

"Yes, it's OK with me."

I looked at Ed and Peter. They *had* to have that boat, at almost any price. And now they wanted to give her away.

I didn't try to understand.

19. Lucifer

Blowing in from the Bering Sea, the storm shook the house. Rain pelted the windows, and wind whistled in the stove. One of the storm doors broke loose and banged in the wind. Ed went to close it and returned to the living room, his hair blown and his shirt spotted with rain. It was nearly midnight.

"A wild night," he said. "I'm going down to drag the skiff above the reach of the surf."

While he was in the kitchen lighting the lantern and pulling on his boots, slicker, and sou'wester, I decided I didn't want to remain alone in the house.

"Wait for me," I called, then ran for my sweater and cap. Ed brought my boots and helped me into my slicker.

The wind nearly swept us off our feet as we stepped into the black night. Lighting an arc about our feet, the lantern helped keep us on the muddy trail that led down the hill through the village and to the beach. Spike walked with his head between us, seeking protection from the wind. On the beach, Ed had to shout to be heard above the roar of the storm and the thunder of the pounding water.

"Look how high the water is. I don't see the boat anywhere."

He held the lantern high trying to locate the little green skiff. The water was a mass of whitecaps and flying spray. Anxiously, Ed walked up and down the beach and into the surf, hoping for a sight of the skiff.

"I'd hate like hell to lose that boat."

After the frightening trip to the *North Star,* I had painted the name *Lucifer* on the skiff and told Ed I could think of many things I'd rather break over her bow than a bottle of champagne.

"Wait till tomorrow when the storm has blown itself out," I suggested. "Peter can help you find her then."

But he was walking up the beach again, scanning the white foam.

Then he shouted, "There she is," and pointed at the little boat bobbing in the waves. He handed me the lantern.

"Stand here and hold this as high as you can."

He rolled up his high boots to his hips and snapped the straps to his belt to hold them up.

"Ed, be careful," I said. "There must be a terrific undertow, and if you slip with those heavy boots, you'll never get up."

He gave me an absent, reassuring nod and started wading through the surf. Spike tried to follow but gave up, shook himself, and stood beside me, whining. Ed waded into water that reached the top of his boots and stood waiting for the wind to swing the skiff on her anchor rope to within his reach.

The lantern hummed, and the sound of the surf reverberated from the cliff behind us. The boat was almost close enough for Ed to reach when, with a sputter, the lamp went out and all was blackness. I screamed to Ed frantically, but my voice was lost in the sound of the wind and waves. I shouted again and again, and waited. The sheltered little bay, usually so familiar and calm, had become strange and savage. I knew Ed would take desperate risks to save his boat.

Minutes dragged by, and I became frantic.

"Ed! Ed!" I shouted, dropping the lantern and running into the surf.

Spike barked at my heels. I shouted again but heard no answer. I slipped on a rock and plunged to my knees, and the cold water ran into my boots. Sobbing, I turned and made my way back up the beach.

At that moment, as I waited helpless and terrified, I hated this wilderness with its storms and isolation and ruggedness. I was shivering, but stood and waited, and waited. Suddenly Spike darted from me into the surf, and I heard Ed shout.

"I'm soaked to my neck, but I got the boat."

Knowing no fear of his own, he was unaware of mine.

Together we dragged the boat over the sand and up to a low ledge on the cliff. Then, helping one another, we emptied the water from our boots. We found the lantern, and Ed put his arm around me to help me up the slippery trail to the station. His mood was buoyant.

"One hell of a storm, isn't it?" he said.

I choked back words better left unsaid and held tightly to his arm.

"Yes. One hell of a storm."

20. Tragedy

When the long shadow of the Depression reached Arctic shores in 1931, fur prices dropped. The price of otter pelts alone—and there were many otters around Kulukak—fell from twenty to ten dollars apiece. The villagers needed money for tea, sugar, cloth, and other provisions from the Outside. The people on the Nushagak needed fresh meat from the Kulukak reindeer herd, so arrangements were made for a small band to be driven there to be sold and butchered. The unsold animals were to be returned to the main herd.

"Must you go?" I asked Ed apprehensively. I thought of the two-day trip over the white tundra in below-zero weather, and I thought of the loneliness in Kulukak awaiting his return.

"I should help all I can," he replied. "I'd like to keep the record of transactions and make sure any remaining deer are brought back."

On a Monday morning in January 1932, the herders drove the deer across the frozen harbor, and the next day they began the long trek to Nushagak. Ed planned to leave Friday and reach Kanakanak about the same time they did.

"If it weren't for your being alone, I'd take Spike," Ed said.

Spike was a quick, alert, and intelligent dog, and Ed had trained him to work as a leader, though he had little endurance.

"If this weather continues, I'll be home a week from today. Hang the lamp in the window if I'm not here by dark."

I stood in the doorway and watched him cross the harbor and disappear from sight. The dogs were fresh and eager to be on the trail. I thought of Anecia, and wished she were with me.

For many nights the lighted lamp hung in the living room window, its beam reaching across the harbor. It was the last light to be extinguished, and that long after midnight.

Two nights after Ed's anticipated return, Spike's growls awakened me, and I heard insistent hammering on the back door. Ed was home! I hurried into my robe and slippers, noticing that the radium dial stood at five o'clock. I hastened through the house, happy at the thought of having my husband home again and those long, lonely days at an end. Sliding the bolt on the storm door, I pushed it open.

In my flashlight beam Evon and the *tyone* stood on the step. Despite Spike's warning growls, they walked past me into the kitchen. I fastened the door and followed. In silence, they stood and watched me. I lighted the kerosene lamp in the wall bracket and felt a vague foreboding.

"Evon," I said, "What do you want?"

He didn't answer. The *tyone* nervously twisted his fur cap. Their shadows trembled on the wall behind them as the flame in the lamp flickered. Finally Evon touched his fur boots and his parka and pointed to me.

"Taitai."

"Come where?"

He didn't answer. Someone in the village must be ill and in need of medical aid, I thought.

"Who, Evon?"

"Mr. Morgan."

Alarm rose within me. "Mr. Morgan? Where?"

He shrugged his shoulders.

"*Cukamek* [hurry], *taitai*."

I motioned for them to sit down, then hurried to the bedroom and got into my clothes. Feeling increasing panic, I whispered a small prayer: "Dear God, don't let anything be wrong with Ed. Anything but that."

The room began to swim, and I refused to let myself think anything was wrong. I was wrought up from the loneliness of the days and nights Ed had been gone, and I trembled because of the chill of the house and because Evon and the *tyone* frightened me. Why had they come? And why hadn't Ed returned two days ago as planned?

I hurried to the kitchen and pulled on my fur boots. I looked up from tying the ankle cords to meet Evon's searching gaze.

"Plenty, plenty cold," he said.

I nodded. I had spent the past week carrying coal and stoking stoves, yet ice still had formed on the water pails in the kitchen, and half the potatoes had frozen. I knew it was bitterly cold.

The men started down the hill, and I followed over crusted snow. Through the half-light of early morning, Eskimos stood in silent groups before their *barabaras*. My apprehension became boundless.

"Oh God, where is Ed?"

Evon led the way to where Madfy, one of the older boys, had harnessed his dogs. Placing a reindeer skin on the basket of the sled, the *tyone* motioned me to get in. Evon took the handlebars, and Madfy and the *tyone* ran beside us.

"Madfy," I shouted. "Where are we going?"

"*Naamikika*. Not far."

"Why are we going?"

"Mr. Morgan."

"Is Mr. Morgan all right?"

"*Non*."

"Why not all right?"

"Too much cold. Mr. Morgan dead."

Dead? No. Ed was all right. He told me he would hurry back. He'd come home to me.

The brake cut through the ice, and the sled slowed to a stop. The *tyone* helped me to my feet. Evon spoke to me, then pointed to a dark figure stretched out on the ice of the bay. I walked to it—to him—alone.

Death to me was my grandfather lying white and still in his gray casket. It was my grandmother softly sobbing and the heavy fragrance of flowers in a closed room. It was hushed voices and the muted tones of an organ.

But here, too, was death. It was Ed lying frozen on the ice of Kulukak Bay. Later that night it was Ed lifeless on a wooden bench in the schoolroom. The blond hair, the square chin that had stubbornly backed up his convictions, the lips that would never again give me the crooked smile. I sank into deep darkness.

Excited whispers came closer to me in the crowded room. My head felt as if it were being crushed. Evon, on his knees, rubbed his hand over my forehead, and I pushed it away and sat up. I got to my feet and into a chair. After a little while, I went to the bedroom for a blanket, and tenderly I covered Ed's body.

The villagers, my only friends in this vast wilderness, stood watching me. Ocalena and Sophia sobbed. What does a person do when a loved one dies?

After daybreak, Madfy pulled my arm. "Come," he said, pointing in the direction of the bay. "We found dogs and sled."

"Madfy, tell Evon to send somebody for help, to Nushagak or Togiak," I said.

They talked together in Yup'ik.

"No dogs," Madfy said to me. "No sled. All at Nushagak with reindeer."

"But they took me to Ed by dogsled that morning."

Madfy shook his head. "Old sled. Broken. Dogs no good."

He pointed again to the harbor. "Come now for sled and dogs."

I looked at the people in the room. They were deeply concerned but helpless.

"Madfy, tell them I want them to leave now. Maybe later help me."

I followed Madfy and the *tyone* down the hill, out onto the bay. In the vast blue and white silence there was only the sound of crunching ice beneath our feet. The mountain loomed tall and white and rugged. In this beautiful land, how could there be such sorrow? We had plodded along a mile or more when the *tyone* stopped suddenly, touched my arm, and signaled to listen. We heard the faint but unmistakable drone of an airplane. I prayed that it would come close enough for the pilot to see three specks on the bay, and we could signal it. We could form a letter "T," the distress signal. The engine noise came closer, and Madfy was the first to see it in the cloudless sky. Barely visible, it flew toward Nushagak.

Madfy shook his head. "No come," he said, and he and the *tyone* walked on. The plane and the drone of its engine faded away, and with it went hope. Nothing would come, nobody from my world. In dark despair, I followed the two men farther out onto the bay.

We had walked perhaps two miles when we found the dogs and the sled at the foot of a cliff. A glance at Ed's frosted discarded clothes told the heartbreaking story. He had been in water to his waist. The bowed front end of the sled, the runners, and half the stanchions were coated with ice. The sleeping bag, open on the floor of the sled, had been occupied. The gasoline stove and a box of unopened matches were nearby with the suitcase and mailbag. The unlighted matches and the unopened suitcase told the grim tale of fingers too frozen to move, unable to light the stove or open the suitcase for dry clothes. Desperate he had abandoned his gear and his dogs and started for home.

The dogs huddled together. Tony and Rowdy jumped to their feet and whined. Judy stood on trembling legs. I told Madfy to wrap her and put her in the sled.

The canvas case of Ed's prized new .22 caliber rifle was coated with ice. His gloves, frozen stiff, lay on the ice, fingers up, and his windbreaker was in a frozen, wrinkled heap. The two men and I gathered the gear and loaded it on the sled. Madfy drove the dogs as the *tyone* and I followed him back to the village.

The night before, Ed had been there alone, returning by the same route he had taken to Nushagak. But one day while he was gone, a terrific tide backed by heavy winds had lifted a section of the harbor ice and carried it out to sea. New ice had formed, thinner than before, and as Ed had driven over it with his sled, it had given way. Somehow, perhaps because the tide was out and the water shallow, he had managed to save his dogs and sled.

I remembered that at a little after three that morning Spike had awakened me by whining at the door. I let him out, and for a long time he didn't come when I called him. Could he have heard Ed? When the atmosphere was right in cold, clear weather and the snow crusted, from up at the station we could hear footsteps on the harbor ice. Because I was alone and Ed had been gone longer than he had anticipated, perhaps he had traveled all night.

Back at the station, Madfy staked out the dogs. I gave him the key to the warehouse where Ed stored the dried fish and asked him to feed the dogs well. I took Judy to the coal shed, made her a bed of reindeer hides, and fed her warm milk and bread.

The men brought Ed's belongings to the kitchen. I removed the gun from its case and put it on a chair where the ice melted and water dripped from the barrel. Carefully, I cleaned and oiled it.

"Keep busy," I thought. "Don't stop. Don't think."

The frozen clothes lost their angular stiffness and hung limply. I laid the stack of letters, the magazines, and the box of candy on the desk.

This couldn't be true. I thought of the wife of the teacher whose grave was on the hill. Had she been as alone as I?

Evon and Madfy came in.

"I have to have help," I told them.

"Maybe pretty soon men and reindeer come from Nushagak."

"But I need help now. Take our dogs and sled."

Evon shook his head. "Not take Schoolarista's team. Mr. Morgan dead."

Their superstitions wouldn't allow them to take anything that had belonged to Ed. They went back outside and began to carry a long box made of rough lumber into the schoolroom. I thought of Baby Matrona, of Maluk, of the graves in the frozen ground, and of the finality.

"No! No! Take it away. Evon, take it out. Put it back in the carpenter shack. Not yet. Not yet."

I closed the door and locked it. Through the long, long night I walked the floor and sat numbly in the schoolroom.

At daybreak Ocalena came to the station. I sent her for Evon, Madfy, and the *tyone,* and they came immediately.

"Madfy, tell them I *have* to have help. Someone has to leave for Togiak right away."

"Too much storm," came the reply. "No dogs."

I became frantic, then said suddenly, "I'll go. I'll take Spike, and we'll follow the tripods."

They left, Evon shaking his head with concern. I gathered my heavy clothes while Ocalena stood by wringing her hands.

"No go alone!" she said. "No! No!"

Then she called me to the window, and we saw Wassilia with the old sled and five dogs making his way up the hill. Lucy came to the door. A team had gone for help.

All that day, all that night, until late the next afternoon I sat beside Ed. I waited at the window, watching the trail. The girls, frightened and superstitious, were no comfort to me. Spike and I remained alone.

In her hour of need, my grandmother had turned to her religion. She said that God was her help and that He watched over all of us. But I was blinded by bitterness. Where was God when Ed went through the ice? And where was He when Baby Matrona needed help and when Maluk lay ill and suffering? I put down the Bible my grandmother had given me. I didn't pray. I felt forsaken and forgotten.

On the evening of the third day, during a heavy snowstorm, four teams arrived from Togiak. Mr. Schrammeck questioned the wisdom of my decision that Ed be buried at Kulukak. But I was sure I would not regret it. During the last few days, my thoughts had gone back to Ed's statement after Mace's death that he wouldn't have wanted his body shipped Outside. And I remembered a summer afternoon when Ed and I, returning from a walk, rested on a hill near the grave of the first teacher who had come to Kulukak.

I remarked, "There's something pitifully lonely about that grave."

Ed disagreed. "I'd rather be buried here in the quiet solitude than anywhere Outside."

21. Alone

The next morning Mr. Schrammeck left for Kana-kanak to send the sad message to our families and to the Juneau office. He planned to be gone four days, but was overtaken by severe snowstorms and bitter winds. On the evening of the sixth day, over radio station KFQD, came the message that he was at Kanakanak waiting for a break in the weather. Ten days after he left, we saw his team returning across the bay. He brought telegrams from our families, including one from Cousin Edgar, expressing shock and sorrow and strong opposition to my plan to remain in Kulukak until spring. There were messages from our friends at Kanakanak and telegrams from government officials. Three men from the Juneau office would come within two weeks to make arrangements for me. The doctor was to come as soon as weather permitted.

Despite the loneliness, I wanted to complete the year's work at Kulukak, to take our belongings and Spike out with me, and to dispose of other things, such as the sled, guns, and radio, and, above, all, to leave Ed's grave as it always would be. It had no marker, not even a cross, and Mr. Schrammeck planned to place a cement slab over it in the spring.

I needed to know that I had left the village with my work complete, that there was nothing that remained to be done and nothing for which to return.

So there he should rest, in the country he loved, beside the grave of the teacher. On January 30, in the dusky grayness and frozen silence of late afternoon, Mr. Schrammeck stood beside the canvas-covered box that rested on the couch in the living room. Peter, Chris, Evon, the *tyone* and other villagers stood near the door. By the window, Mrs. Schrammeck read in a soft, low voice Psalm 91, my grandmother's favorite. Numb with sorrow, I stood at the head of the box, lifted the corner of the white linen handkerchief, and looked for the last time at my Ed.

Mrs. Schrammeck put down the Bible, and her husband slid the cover of the box up and tightened the screws. I walked behind the sled as the men pushed it up the hill. Gently, with ropes, they lowered the casket between the walls of frozen brown earth. Then with tears blurring the trail, I turned and made my way back down the hill to the station.

Life is this: To walk a windy night while men are dying,
To cry for one to come, and none to heed our crying.

John Masefield

I wondered what to do with the sled dogs—big, clumsy, lovable Tony, quiet old gentleman Jumbo, Judy, and the younger ones. To give them to the Eskimos was unthinkable because of their superstitions about a dead person's possessions. No one answered when I asked my question because the answer was obvious.

Choking back tears of bitterness, I turned from the window as Mr. Schrammeck drove Ed's dogs—with the

Ed's grave. In the background is the grave of the first Kulukak
teacher, who died in 1912.

exception of the two pups, Balder and Turpie—over the hills to be shot.

Mr. Schrammeck returned to Togiak while his wife and Wallace remained with me for a time. He took Balder, who was more house pet than sled dog because of his short hair, and I planned to keep Turpie as long as I could before giving him also to Mr. Schrammeck. I kept busy from morning to night and was grateful for the quiet presence of Mrs. Schrammeck. My twenty-fifth birthday came and went, unnoticed and unobserved.

One afternoon a plane flew over, circled low, and landed on the ice of the bay. Three government officials, dressed in furs from head to foot, made their way up the trail. Because of my desire to remain in the village until spring, they made arrangements for me to continue teaching and complete the reindeer records. After looking over the station, the springhouse, and the warehouse, the men reboarded the plane.

Early one morning Peter, with thirteen dogs in harness, left with Mrs. Schrammeck and Wallace for Togiak. Loneliness, deep and desolate, settled over me as I turned back to the empty house. All day in the schoolroom I kept busy, not even returning to the living quarters for lunch. To avoid being alone, I kept the school youngsters an hour longer than usual, then invited the older girls to come and sew in the evening. Ocalena was last to leave after school, and I fought a flood of sadness as she prepared to depart.

"Now I go" was her way of saying good-bye. She had no mother, no home, and no one to really take care of her. She and her younger sister, Sophia, lived with old Anuska. When their mother died giving birth to Sophia, the baby had been placed beside the mother's body for burial. Childless Anuska, sister of the dead woman, begged for the baby. The father gave it to her, but he never showed kindness or affection to the motherless

Kulukak in winter. The fish caches and kayaks are out of the dogs' reach.

child. Once I had to send word to Anuska that Sophia's fur boots needed mending because gunny sack strips were all that protected the child's toes from the cold.

"Ocalena," I said suddenly, "would you like to stay with me for a while?"

"*Aang, aang*" was her reply. "I much like to stay with you."

"Go get your clothes, tell Anuska, then come back."

A few minutes later she returned, placed her small bundle on the floor, and removed her parka.

"Ocalena, I'm lonely. You'll talk with me, won't you?"

She nodded. "I try hard to learn English."

That night she bathed in the washtub and shampooed her hair.

"Ocalena, are there bugs in your clothes?"

"Maybe little bugs," she said, and we dipped them in antiseptic and washed them well. She put on a pair of my pajamas and helped me make her bed on the living room couch.

Ocalena tried her best to help and to talk with me, and I was increasingly pleased to have her. But in one respect she couldn't be changed. She couldn't be reasoned out of her superstitions. She shut and locked doors long before dark, and often she ran into my room in the small hours of the night.

"Schoolarista, I scared," she would say.

"What of?"

"A *carayak* keeps making a noise."

"It's the rope whipping the flagpole in the wind."

"No! *Carayak* not in front. He in coal shed."

The next day I investigated and found the cause. It was a fifty-gallon gasoline drum painted green like the station standing outside the coal shed. In the spring and fall it caught rainwater, and the bottom had bulged from water freezing in it. When a strong wind blew, the drum rocked on its rounded base, and it occasionally bumped against the shed wall.

The days dragged by, and the nights were lonely eternities. I held school on Saturdays, and the children would have come on Sundays as well, and stayed until bedtime if I had let them.

The doctor and the game warden arrived one afternoon with two teams and a guide. The doctor held a clinic for the villagers, and gave each child and young adult diphtheria serum. On the party's return from Togiak, he vaccinated the children for smallpox. Instructed to make a complete investigation into Ed's death, the doctor asked endless questions.

Late one afternoon, a team crossed the harbor, and as it came up the hill I went outside to meet it. The sun was shining, and the passenger, a Caucasian woman, had pushed back her parka hood, so that I could see her white hair. She was waving, and for a moment I was certain it was my mother. I ran toward the sled, but quick tears of disappointment filled my eyes when I realized it was a woman I had never seen before.

I apologized and the white-haired woman introduced herself as the government dentist, saying that she had never called at a station where she had been so warmly welcomed. She stayed in Kulukak for several days, caring for the children's teeth, and then her guide took her on to Togiak.

Mr. Schrammeck came through on his way to Dillingham. Over the Bethel broadcast he had received a message instructing him to go there as soon as possible to send a detailed statement of Ed's accident to be forwarded to Washington, D.C. He was also to give the children their second inoculation of smallpox vaccine.

The morning he left was clear and cold with a beautiful blue sky and heavily crusted snow, a good day to travel.

"A mail plane has been in to Nushagak since anyone has come this way," he said. "There should be some mail there for you."

Mr. Schrammeck adjusted the fur hood around his face and pulled on his shaggy, well-worn mittens.

"Say, that dog of yours is keen to be on the trail. Better keep him inside for a couple of hours."

I nodded. "But he'd never run away."

Mr. Schrammeck stepped off the brake and signaled the waiting, eager dogs to be off. Inside the house, Spike whined and ran from one door to the other, then put his paws on the window sill and whined some more. Mr. Schrammeck and his team were barely visible in the distance. He was off to a good start. I hoped the weather wouldn't change.

Recess came, and the youngsters ran outside. Stephan stood beside the desk and asked, "Please, Spike he play with me?"

"He's in the living quarters," I said. "You go get him."

I thought no more about Spike until after recess, when the children were in their seats and I glanced out at the bay. A dog moved across the ice.

"Oh no," I cried. "Stephan, where's Spike?"

"*Naamikika.*"

I ran to the door and called, but I knew that the dog out on the ice was Spike. I picked him up through the binoculars running between the parallel tracks left by the sled runners. It was useless to call, useless to ring the bell, useless to fire a gun. And it was also useless to try to overtake him. He traveled at a swift gait, with his nose to the ground and his tail curled up over his back. Spike loved the excitement of life on the trail, and he had gone in search of it.

Heartsick, I knew I might never see him again. Fox traps were cunningly set this time of year, and sometimes poison was spread, unlawfully, for furbearing animals. Also, Spike couldn't endure the cold as the malamutes could, and soon his feet would be cut and bleeding from the crusted snow.

And he wouldn't be curled on the reindeer rug beside my bed at night. I liked knowing he was there. His presence made the world a less lonely place.

That evening the older girls of the village came up to the station, and we popped corn on the range and sewed. They loved to come, and I was only too happy to have them. I made many trips to the back door, thinking I heard Spike. Surely, I thought, he would turn back when he got hungry and cold or his feet became tender. In the night, when Ocalena thought she heard *carayaks,* I thought I heard Spike. But two days and two nights

Stephan and Spike

went by with no sign of him. I had sent word through the village, hoping a traveler might find him and bring him home.

The third afternoon, a messenger from Togiak came to the door and handed me a letter from Mrs. Schrammeck.

"My husband sent this message over the Bethel broadcast: 'Arrived Kanakanak. Spike overtook me on the trail. If possible, send word to Mrs. Morgan.' "

The days became less empty and desolate. Within a week, thin, limping Spike, almost too weary to wag his tail, dragged into the house while Mr. Schrammeck unharnessed his team and staked the dogs. For three days Spike scarcely left his bed behind the kitchen range. His sole interest was to rest, soak up the warmth, and lick his cracked, bleeding foot pads.

The mailbag of letters Mr. Schrammeck brought into the kitchen was a welcome sight. From many of them I found comfort. One said, "Remember, it's better to lose than to never have had," and another said, "Be grateful you had those wonderful years together." I understood those sentiments because my memories were rich, and they gave me courage to go on. But the letter that said, "You are young. You'll forget, for time heals all things" left me with a bitter lump in my throat. I was young, but that gave me years to live with this deep hurt inside me. And how could I ever forget?

When the people of Kulukak left for the summer seal camps and the ice began going out of the bay, I went by dogsled with Mr. Schrammeck to Togiak to stay until after the breakup and the arrival of the *North Star,* when we would return to Kulukak by boat for my trunks. The trail was heavy from fresh snow, and pulling was hard for the dogs. Mr. Schrammeck consented to let me walk up a steep hill, but I was glad to crawl back in the sled when we reached the top. Sometimes as we came along a riverbank, we looked ahead to where high tides had raised, then taken out the ice over the channel, leaving a steep wall of ice. The flats, in the afternoon sun, were covered with water. Occasionally we saw a herd of reindeer.

I thought again of the lines from "The Spell of the Yukon," by Robert Service that Cousin Edgar had quoted to Grandmother.

> The strong life that never knows harness
> The wilds where the caribou call,
> The freshness, the freedom, the farness,
> Oh God, how I'm stuck on it all!

Spike trotted behind us, and Turpie lumbered along with an elephant's gait, refusing to be hurried.

Peter made the trip to Togiak before dogsled travel became impossible, bringing me a letter written on soiled, crumpled paper, in little George's pinched, uphill handwriting.

Dear Morgan.
   Please come back, Mrs. Morgan. I like to go to school.
                                                    Your friend,
                                                    George

I sent an answer to my little first grader and later learned of his boundless joy and pride in receiving it. He carried it about in the pocket of his jeans and read it so often that it finally fell apart at the folds.

One afternoon at Togiak I answered a tap on the back door. If the man's coat and cap had been red, and if his team had been reindeer instead of three scrawny dogs, I'd have been certain it was Santa Claus. But his fur-bare parka was torn and ragged, and his cap partially covered taffy-gold blond hair that hung in ringlets to his shoulders. His beard reached below his waist. He pulled off his cap, but before I could speak, Mr. Schrammeck walked up.

"Could you let me have some fish for my dogs?" the man asked.

"Come in. Come in," Mr. Schrammeck said. The man stomped the snow from his feet and stepped inside.

After he fed his dogs, the old prospector sat at the kitchen table hungrily consuming hot food. In clipped, half-sentences, he talked as he ate.

"Haven't seen a white man for nearly three years. Found good rock east of here. Been damned sick. Have to see a doctor. Maybe go Outside. Bad time last winter, caught out in the mountains. Thought my legs were frozen. If they had been, I'd have shot my dogs and myself."

He stood and pushed in his chair. "Sure grateful for the grub and the dog food. Nice of you to give it to me. Kinda short on money."

We watched the man disappear over the tundra and wondered if he could get through to Kanakanak before ice went out of the rivers and creeks. Huge cakes of ice were piled up on the beach of Togiak Harbor, and the blue waters were dotted with floes.

Spring was coming again to the northland.

22. Farewell

I waited at the edge of the ice-rimmed bay, watching the men lift my trunks and boxes into the sailboat. A five-foot wall of ice still rimmed the shores of Kulukak Bay. I had just come from the hillside, where, for the last time, I stood beside Ed's grave.

In that remote Eskimo village, our home for two wonderful years, we had known extreme happiness, and I had known deepest sorrow. I was returning to Togiak to await the arrival of the *North Star,* which would take me back to the States and my family.

Lost and lonely, I walked over to the warehouse. I remembered the happy hours we had spent as Ed worked on the building and I perched on the pile of lumber chatting with him. Later, dressed in slacks, I had slid along the roof and laid the shingles while he followed and nailed them. It was part of a beautiful story with a sad, sad ending. Now I was to leave, alone.

I walked back to the edge of the ice. The fresh red blood of a seal who had met his end while he bobbed among the ice floes earlier that morning spotted the pure white.

The boats were ready. Chris and Mr. Schrammeck were in the dory with the motor, and Peter, Ocalena, and I were in the sailboat. There was little wind, so Mr. Schrammeck and Chris planned to tow our boat. The sudden throb of the engine broke the silence.

Peter stood in the stern puffing his pipe while I sat on my steamer trunk. Ocalena was close beside me, quiet and thoughtful. I longed to bury my head in my arms and give way to the hurt inside me. Life was wrong that I should leave Kulukak alone and that Ed's grave was up on the hill. I tried not to think.

Peter took the pipe from his mouth.

"You won't always feel as you do now," he said. "Outside you'll be with your family and friends. It won't be so hard."

He was trying to help me, but I didn't believe him. He called my attention to an eagle that soared above a jagged rock ledge at the point of the headland.

"Its nest is at the top of that cliff. It robs the nests of ducks and ptarmigan, and is a terror to birds and animals on the tundra," he said.

As we left the bay, I looked back. I tried to memorize it all so as to keep with me always those precious pictures. With a lonely, faraway feeling, I watched Kulukak drop from sight.

"The wind's changing, and the weather doesn't look good," Peter said to me. "We're going to have a hard trip."

He said that when we stopped at Herring Bay, the summer seal camp, to drop off Ocalena, we should pick up Evon so we would have two men in each boat. Before the day was over, I realized the wisdom of his suggestion.

As we entered the inlet at the summer camp, Evon drifted motionless in his kayak, stalking seals. Peter signaled to him to follow us to camp. When our boats neared the beach, the people—men, women, and children—gathered at the shore.

"Peter," I said, "I want to go ashore and see them, tell them good-bye."

While Mr. Schrammeck put gasoline in the engine, and Peter and Chris sat on their heels in front of a low tent, eating seal meat, I stood on the beach and talked with the youngsters. Ocalena, I knew, was deeply saddened at my leaving. When she had learned that I was at Kulukak, she immediately set out from summer camp to see me, walking alone many miles over the tundra. She now whispered, "You most wonderful white lady," and hung her head, not raising it or waving as I climbed into the sailboat. George and a boy named Yukeyak ran along the beach waving until they became tiny specks against the snow.

A strong headwind blew up, and it was all the motor could do to pull the sailboat. The men tried tacking into the wind with the dory still pulling. Both boats were taking in water in the rough seas. Evon bailed in our boat, Chris in the dory. Spray flew over the bow and soaked us. When lifted on a swell, the dory's bow rose high in the air. Mr. Schrammeck was a poor sailor, and I knew how he hated rough water.

Chris unrolled his *qalirtaq* and slipped it over his parka. Peter told me that one walrus gut, washed, blown up, and dried, then slit lengthwise, was long enough to make two or three such raincoats. One strip ran from the wrist, up over the head, and down to the other wrist. It was pieced about the hood and arms, running spirally, beginning at the top of the hood, around and around until the desired hip length was reached. There were drawstrings at the wrists, the face, and about the bottom. Large and loose, it fitted over the kayak opening, enabling a hunter to be safe in the stormiest weather. If his kayak turned over, no water got in before he had it righted again. The *qalirtaq* was transparent and served as a windbreak as well as a raincoat.

Beyond the seal camp, around the point from Herring Bay on the tundra, with no other rocks or brush around it, stood a tall, lonely stone. Peter told me that Eskimo legend claimed it was a young mother with her baby on her back. One day, long ago, when the sea was rough and the winds high, her husband went seal hunting. Uneasy and anxious, the young wife, with her baby, followed along the beach, watching her husband. With horror, she saw his kayak capsize in the rough water and watched him disappear in the depths. She turned to stone and still keeps her lonely vigil. Beyond, toward Owen's place, are marks on a rock where she sat waiting, and the baby's footprints can be seen on the stone where he stood leaning against her back. Beyond this rock is another, smooth and flat, bearing her fingerprints.

Peter emptied his pipe over the water and stuffed it in his pocket.

"We're making no headway and using a hell of a lot of gasoline and getting wetter every minute."

He lowered the sail and motioned to Mr. Schrammeck and Chris. They shut off the engine and drifted alongside the sailboat. They decided it was useless to buck the wind and tide. We would seek shelter for the night in a nearby inlet, Coffee Cove. Peter explained that he and Chris gave the inlet its name twenty years before on a trip from Kulukak to Togiak.

"We got caught in a storm and had to run for shelter in this inlet. We were cold and made coffee, and ever since we've called it Coffee Cove."

But I felt it had been misnamed. It was a beautiful place, a little half circle of blue water surrounded by a sandy beach with rock precipices rising above. A slender waterfall splashed over a cliff. At the far end, waves broke against a rock reef, and spray flew in white mist. Peter remarked that the reef was good hunting ground for seals.

We dropped anchor, hauled up the motor, and fastened the boats together. Peter made coffee in the battered old kettle over the little gasoline stove. Soon the fresh aroma of coffee blended with the smoke of his pipe.

Mr. Schrammeck refused the steaming cup offered him. But the oily surface of the dark liquid and the unscoured kettle didn't spoil that hot coffee for me. I was cold and wet and hungry. Chris grinned when I eagerly accepted a second cup. My thoughts, as he poured it, were of another time when I had tasted cod cooked in seawater in that same kettle.

Next came the problem of our being as warm and comfortable as possible for the night. Mr. Schrammeck and Peter cleared a space for me in the bow of the sailboat, but even though I was dressed in furs and tucked into a down sleeping bag, I still shivered. An Arctic gale whipped the boats all night long. Lying awake, I thought of my father, who, that day, May 2, was celebrating his birthday. It was well that he did not know where his daughter was that night.

I listened to the nearby gentle lapping of the outgoing tide and to the distant thunder of surf pounding the reef. My tears blurred the boat's mast and the stars overhead. The last time I had been in Peter's boat, Ed and I were curled together in the sleeping bag, and, though we were cold, we laughed at the narrow bag that forced us to sleep spoon-style, both of us either on our left sides or on our right. I tried to plan ahead, to think of the days to come, but could see only endless, bleak loneliness.

Gradually, the sky lightened, and the men came to life. My breath made little puffs of fog as I crawled from the sleeping bag and looked around. Shell ice had formed on the surface of the water, the ropes were coated, and icicles hung from the gunwales of the boats.

Once more, I drank strong black coffee and consumed a hard, dry sandwich.

Between bites, Chris said, "We can't travel today. Still got a strong headwind."

Peter and Evon decided to hunt seal on the reef, and Mr. Schrammeck and I walked on the beach to keep warm. After a while, I sat on the rocks and watched the waves break over the reef. Mr. Schrammeck scanned the skies.

"I doubt very much if we'll travel tomorrow, either."

The thought of being anchored all day, another night, and perhaps even another day and night, walking the beach to keep warm, was unbearable.

"How far is it to Togiak?" I asked.

"Perhaps fifteen miles as the crow flies. A good twenty-mile hike."

"Is it possible to hike it now?"

"Creeks would have to be waded, but it could be done."

"My heavy boots are at Togiak."

"I could carry you across the creeks."

"Let's try to make it."

Mr. Schrammeck stood looking at me. I knew he was thinking that I was pale, thin, and immersed in grief. He wondered how much endurance I would have. He was afraid to start the trip with me.

"I can make it," I said.

He shook his head. "It's a hard trip for a strong man. But waiting here is hard, too. There's a shelter, Owen's place, midway between here and Togiak. If necessary, we could stop there overnight."

"I know I can make it."

He went to the reef to tell Chris and Peter of our intentions. They came back with him, and the four of us returned to the sailboat. While Mr. Schrammeck got some lunch to take with us, I reached into my trunk for wool socks and my old moccasin walking shoes. Chris shook his head.

"That's too rough a trip for you, but you'll *never* make it in those."

"I'm going to take my mukluks, too," I told him.

The flat, smooth-soled fur boots of the Eskimos tired

me, but I stuffed extra wool socks inside them, tied the drawstrings together, and slung them over my shoulder.

With misgivings, Chris and Peter watched us leave. To break the tension, I called back, "I'll be on the beach when you reach Togiak."

Never was walking such hard work. Sometimes on crusted snow that held us, sometimes breaking through and dropping to our knees, hips, or even our waists in the soft snow, we slogged over hummocks and through snowdrifts. The best walking was along the beach for short stretches.

Mr. Schrammeck insisted that I take the lead and set the pace. We plodded along, mile after mile, with only snow-blanketed tundra ahead, behind, and to the east of us. Off to the west was the blue of the Bering Sea. The only signs of life were ptarmigan darting through the air, calling to their mates with a clipped "Come here. Come here."

Some time past noon we reached the shelter, the old home of a white man named Owen, who many years before had married an Eskimo woman. Owen and his wife had died leaving nine children to shift for themselves. Paddy, a youth of twenty, was the oldest and the provider. During the winter months the family lived in Togiak with relatives and attended school.

When we knocked at the door of the weather-beaten frame house, a teenage boy warmly welcomed us. The five younger children—two girls (the oldest and the youngest of the group) and three boys, one a hunchback—stood before us, eagerly interested, and smiling as we talked. They gave us boxes to sit on in the bare, dark little kitchen while the oldest boy made us coffee.

I hung my wet socks on a sagging rope over the old range, and Mr. Schrammeck and I shared our cheese, Ry Krisp, and raisins with the children. After an hour's rest, I pulled on my dry, warm socks and we said good-bye to those lost, lonely children.

We now faced a bitter north wind. Miles beyond Owen's place my pace began to slacken, and more and more often it was necessary to stop for a moment's rest. My back screamed with pain from walking braced against the strong wind. Even to breathe was an effort.

"We're about halfway between Owen's place and Togiak," Mr. Schrammeck said. "There's some bad stretches ahead. Think you can make it?"

I nodded.

"If you walk close behind me, perhaps I can break the force of the wind."

That was better, but still I lagged behind in the relentless wind. When I fell, tears of weariness and rising despair filled my eyes. Once, as we stopped for a minute, Mr. Schrammeck suggested that he go ahead and return for me with his team and sled. Unreasoning fear gripped me. I knew no harm would befall me in this beautiful land I loved, but in the dark, away from Kulukak, I didn't want to be left alone.

We trudged on mile after mile, stopping to rest when I could go no farther. As the black night enveloped us, fear that perhaps I wasn't going to make it after all consumed me. With utter despair, I realized Mr. Schrammeck would have to go ahead. Fearfully, I asked, "How much farther?"

"Before long we should see the light of the station."

These words spurred me on, and long after dark we plodded into the village, with the malamutes announcing our arrival.

Mrs. Schrammeck greeted her husband with as much delight as Spike welcomed me. He pulled at my gloves with his teeth, and when I dropped into a chair his forepaws instantly were in my lap. His plaintive whimpers voiced the feelings I had within myself.

Mrs. Schrammeck helped me out of my heavy clothes, and with the deepest exhaustion I had ever known, I crawled into bed, with Spike curled up on the floor nearby, and slipped into the blessed oblivion of sleep.

Early the following afternoon, the dory and sailboat appeared in the harbor. Peter and Chris came immediately to the station and were obviously relieved when they saw me.

Peter grinned, "Damned if I ever thought you'd make it. We bucked the wind all the way to get here. Thought we'd take a team and head for Owen's place. Was sure you'd be there."

The days dragged by as I watched the horizon, hoping each morning that before the sun set that night the *North Star* would come. Spike and I spent hours each day tramping over the tundra or walking along the beach. My eyes constantly, hopefully, scanned the harbor entrance.

Then, early one morning, a villager pounded on the door. He pointed out to the horizon, and there, where the sky met the Bering Sea, was the *North Star,* waiting for the flood tide. She was the ship that was to take me back to the States and to my family.

Epilogue

Abbie returned to teaching in Hoquiam, Washington, where her family lived. Spike had become fiercely protective of her and, with deep regret, she had him put to sleep.

Abbie traveled around the world alone on steamships, then stayed in New York where she did graduate work at Columbia University before returning to Washington.

In 1937 she married Orville Madenwald, whom she had known since childhood. They had two children: Malcolm, an orthopedic surgeon in Washington; and myself, a teacher in California. As the family moved up and down the West Coast following the lumber industry, where Orville was a comptroller, Abbie continued her teaching career. Married forty-eight years, they spent time traveling, enjoying their family, the home they built on the high desert of Oregon, and the dogs they loved.

Abbie never returned to Kulukak, but maintained a close relationship with Ocalena, who taught me to sew my first dress and with whom I continue to share a rewarding friendship.

During 1990, Abbie was delighted to learn she had a

namesake in Bristol Bay. Her student George Ilutsik, one of the boys who herded reindeer, had eventually married and raised a family. Assuming he'd never see his favorite teacher again, he gave the middle name of Abbie to one of his daughters. Esther Abbie Ilutsik became a teacher as well, perhaps encouraged by her father to do so. After finding out about each other, the two became acquainted through correspondence and both enthusiastically made plans to meet personally, but unfortunately that was not to be.

Abbie happily watched her beloved book come to fruition before she passed away in May of 1991.

MARY MADENWALD MCKEOWN